Getting Skills Right

Strengthening Career Guidance for Mid-Career Adults in Australia

OECD
BETTER POLICIES FOR BETTER LIVES

This work is published under the responsibility of the Secretary-General of the OECD. The opinions expressed and arguments employed herein do not necessarily reflect the official views of the Member countries of the OECD.

This document, as well as any data and map included herein, are without prejudice to the status of or sovereignty over any territory, to the delimitation of international frontiers and boundaries and to the name of any territory, city or area.

Please cite this publication as:
OECD (2022), *Strengthening Career Guidance for Mid-Career Adults in Australia*, Getting Skills Right, OECD Publishing, Paris, https://doi.org/10.1787/e08803ce-en.

ISBN 978-92-64-47024-8 (print)
ISBN 978-92-64-56614-9 (pdf)
ISBN 978-92-64-93878-6 (HTML)
ISBN 978-92-64-58115-9 (epub)

Getting Skills Right
ISSN 2520-6117 (print)
ISSN 2520-6125 (online)

Foreword

The world of work is changing. Digitalisation, globalisation, the green transition and population ageing are having a profound impact on the type and quality of jobs that are available and the skills required to perform them. The extent to which individuals, firms and economies can reap the benefits of these changes will depend critically on the readiness of adult learning systems to help people develop and maintain relevant skills over their working careers.

Career guidance for adults is a fundamental policy lever to motivate adults to train and to help address the challenges brought about by rapidly changing skill needs. Such services are particularly important amid the ongoing COVID-19 pandemic and its aftermath, as many adults have lost their job and require assistance in navigating their career options in the rapidly evolving labour market.

To explore this issue, the OECD has undertaken an ambitious programme of work on the functioning, effectiveness and resilience of adult career guidance systems across countries. As part of this project, the OECD carried out an online survey in 11 countries (Australia, Argentina, Brazil, Canada, Chile, Mexico, New Zealand, France, Germany, Italy, and the United States) between 2020 and 2021 to better understand the user experience of adults with career guidance, and any barriers adults might face in accessing these services. The OECD also prepared a policy questionnaire to collect information on good practices across OECD countries in the area of career guidance for adults.

This report provides a review of career guidance for mid-career adults in Australia. Chapter 1 discusses trends affecting the demand for skills in Australia, and presents international survey evidence on the use of career guidance among mid-career adults. Chapter 2 examines what constitutes high-quality career guidance for mid-career adults by looking at how career guidance services should be delivered, how to motivate mid-career adults to seek out career guidance, who should provide the services, and how to fund them. Chapter 3 provides an assessment of the current policy co-ordination and service provision for career guidance for mid-career adults in Australia, and makes recommendations on how they could be improved. In addition to new survey evidence, the report's analysis draws on virtual interviews with Australian stakeholders.

Dzana Topalovic and Katharine Mullock from the Skills and Employability Division of the Directorate for Employment, Labour and Social Affairs are the authors of this report. Erika Xiomara Chaparro Pérez provided valuable statistical research. The work was carried out under the supervision of Glenda Quintini (Manager of the Skills Team) and Mark Keese (Head of the Skills and Employability Division) and benefited from helpful contributions from members of the Skills team. Special thanks are due to the many Australian stakeholders for sharing their expertise and insights during virtual interviews between July and September 2021.

This report is published under the responsibility of the Secretary General of the OECD, with the financial assistance of the Australian Department of Education, Skills and Employment. The views expressed in this report should not be taken to reflect the official position of OECD member countries.

Table of contents

FIGURES

Follow OECD Publications on:

http://twitter.com/OECD_Pubs

http://www.facebook.com/OECDPublications

http://www.linkedin.com/groups/OECD-Publications-4645871

http://www.youtube.com/oecdilibrary

http://www.oecd.org/oecddirect/

Acronyms and abbreviations

ABS	The Australian Bureau of Statistics
ANZSCO	The Australian and New Zealand Standard Classification of Occupations
AUD	Australian dollar
CBQ	Competence-based qualification
CEAV	Career Education Association of Victoria
CEP	Conseil en Evolution Professionelle (France)
CICA	Career Industry Council of Australia
COVID-19	Coronavirus disease 2019
CPP	Career Pathway Plan
CTA	Career Transition Assistance
DESE	The Department of Education, Skills and Employment
EUR	Euro
EUWIN	The European Workforce Innovation Network
HILDA	The Household, Income and Labour Dynamics in Australia Survey
HR	Human Resources
ICTC	Information and Communication Technology Council (Canada)
ILO	International Labour Organization
ISCO	International Standard Classification of Occupations
JVCCS	Jobs Victoria Career Counsellor Services
NCI	National Careers Institute
NSW	New South Wales
OCWI	Ontario Centre for Workforce Innovation (Canada)
OECD	Organisation for Economic Co-operation and Development
O*NET	The Occupational Information Network
PES	Public Employment Services
PIAAC	The Programme for the International Assessment of Adult Competencies
RPL	Recognition of prior learning
SCGA	Survey of Career Guidance for Adults
SMEs	Small and medium-sized enterprises
STEP	Skills, Training and Employment Plan
TAFEs	Technical and Further Education Institutions
VET	Vocational Education and Training

Executive summary

The demand for skills has undergone significant change across OECD countries over the past few decades in response to automation, population ageing, globalisation, and more recently with the COVID-19 pandemic and the ongoing transition to a green economy. In such a rapidly changing world of work, adults in Australia are being challenged to upskill, retrain and consider alternative career paths. Mid-career individuals are in a unique position to take advantage of these changes: they have acquired considerable skills and experience but still have many years left in the labour market before retirement. However, to leverage these advantages, they could benefit from the help of a career professional in navigating this changing labour market and identifying suitable retraining and upskilling opportunities to remain productive and satisfied at work.

This study reviews the career guidance programmes currently available for mid-career adults in Australia and puts these programmes into international perspective. It relies on evidence from the OECD Survey of Career Guidance for Adults (SCGA), carried out in 11 countries during 2020-21, and virtual interviews with key Australian stakeholders.

Mid-career adults in Australia use career guidance services more than those in other countries in the survey. According to the SCGA, 56% of Australian mid-career adults used a career guidance service at least once in the past five years, more than the survey average (38%). An important caveat is that a large share of survey respondents report receiving career support from publicly funded employment services (whether federally funded or state-funded), and most of these services focus on job matching rather than career guidance. Mid-career Australians are also more likely to receive career guidance through their employer than mid-career adults in other countries. This may partially explain why mid-career adults in Australia are more likely to use career guidance to progress in their current employment (43%) (for which employer-provided guidance is most pertinent) than to transition to new jobs or industries (32%). Career guidance that is not offered through one's employer is better placed to support those who wish to change job or industry; but career guidance is rarely available publicly in Australia and private services are used much less in Australia than elsewhere. Australia does not offer financial incentives to support co-funding of private career guidance, and has a higher rate of out-of-pocket payment for services.

Mid-career adults who could arguably most benefit from career guidance use it the least: adults in part-time employment, low-educated adults, women, those living in rural areas, or foreign-born adults are much less likely to use career guidance than their counterparts, and these gaps in usage are higher in Australia than elsewhere. The most common reason for not using career guidance services was not feeling the need (56%), while 20% of mid-career adults did not know such services existed. Women are more likely than men to report lack of time due to family responsibilities as a significant barrier to career guidance. Active outreach can help increase the uptake of vulnerable groups by raising awareness about available services and by highlighting the benefits of career guidance. The state-funded Jobs Victoria is leading the way in this regard. Jobs Victoria Advocates reach out to potentially vulnerable adults in the community (through, for example, libraries and community centres) to connect them with relevant services, including career guidance. Jobs Victoria also trains and employs career guidance advisors who are from similar socio-economic backgrounds as the clients they serve.

Effective career guidance for mid-career adults takes into account skills acquired through informal learning over many years of work experience. It helps them to make these informally acquired skills visible, identifies their transferable skills, maps skills gaps, and creates clear career and training pathways. Australia has several existing programmes that offer such services. However, most are targeted at job seekers (Mid-Career Checkpoint, Skills Checkpoint for Older Workers and Career Transition Assistance programmes), while some target those who are at risk of losing their job (Tasmania's Rapid Response Skills Initiative and the Skills Checkpoint for Older Workers). Moreover, these programmes tend to be offered on a small scale and through employment services by counsellors without specialised training in career guidance.

Employed adults who are not at risk of losing their job do not currently have access to publicly subsidised career guidance in Australia, with the exception of the Jobs Victoria Career Counsellors Service which is open to all adults in Victoria regardless of employment status. In some OECD countries, employed adults can access publicly subsidised career guidance through career vouchers (such as Flanders in Belgium or the Netherlands) or via a dedicated public career guidance service (such as France).

Key recommendations

Strengthen co-ordination of career guidance for mid-career adults

- Raise awareness about available career guidance services, and the benefits of such services for adults at any stage in their career. The National Careers Institute (NCI) could take the lead in these activities.
- Introduce financial support schemes to promote co-funding and reduce the individual cost of private career guidance.
- Strengthen referral systems into and from career guidance services. Stronger referral systems would also help to raise awareness about career guidance services among mid-career adults.

Support mid-career adults facing job disruption or job transition

- Scale up current programmes that target mid-career adults who are employed and at risk of losing their job.
- Support flexible and shorter career and learning pathways for mid-career adults who are facing disruption by better linking career guidance with recognition of prior learning.
- Scale up efforts to reach out to potentially vulnerable adults, such as low-educated adults, those in part-time employment, foreign-born adults, or those living in rural areas, to connect them with career guidance.

Support mid-career adults who are unemployed or out of the labour force

- Scale up publicly provided career guidance programmes that target mid-career jobseekers.
- Require professionals delivering publicly subsidised career guidance programmes to be listed on the Australian Register of Professional Career Development.

Support mid-career adults who are employed and looking to progress in their current job/sector

- Promote the use of high-performance work practices by employers, including flexible and transparent career and learning pathways, job rotation and mentorship programmes. The NCI could take the lead in these activities.
- Expand public provision of career guidance to employed mid-career adults, possibly by extending the current telephone-based career guidance service (School Leavers Information Service) to adults.

1 Why is career guidance for mid-career adults important?

This chapter first looks at trends in the labour market and the demand and supply of skills in Australia. It assesses the degree to which mid-career adults participate in training or change jobs – both possible responses to changing demand for skills. Finally, it reviews survey evidence on the use and inclusiveness of career guidance by mid-career adults in Australia.

In Brief

Mid-career adults in Australia face particular challenges in the current labour market context

The COVID-19 crisis has put pressure on the Australian labour market and amplified existing challenges, especially for some groups most affected by job losses. This has created challenges for mid-career adults who could benefit from career guidance and training opportunities. The key findings of this chapter are outlined as follows:

- Australian adults face a challenging labour market situation after the pandemic. Demand for skills has changed and there is evidence of increasing skills shortages in Australia, more than half of which are concentrated in medium-skilled occupations. The negative employment impacts were most prominent for low-qualified, part-time workers and women, who lost low-skilled jobs and can only take up emerging occupations following retraining.

- Automation and plans to reach zero-carbon emissions by 2050 (hereafter referred to as the green transition) are shifting skills demands in Australia. The COVID-19 pandemic led to an acceleration in the adoption of new technologies. Many of the new jobs created by the green transition will be in medium-skilled occupations, but these may not be located in the same areas where jobs are disappearing.

- Mid-career workers change jobs less often than younger workers. That said, mid-career workers in occupations with high risk of automation change jobs more often than mid-career workers in lower-risk occupations.

- Participation in job-related training is also lower for mid-career adults than for younger adults. Mid-career adults are more likely to participate in training to progress in their current employment – either by improving skills in their current job or maintaining professional status and/or meeting occupation requirements – than with the objective of preparing for a job they might do in the future.

- The share of adults who have spoken to a career guidance advisor is high in Australia compared to other countries covered by the OECD Survey of Career Guidance for Adults (51% vs. 40%) and is particularly high for mid-career adults (56%). An important caveat is that a large share of survey respondents report receiving career support from publicly funded employment services (whether federally funded or state funded), and most of these services focus on job matching rather than career guidance.

- Adults in part-time employment, low-educated adults, women, adults living in rural areas, and foreign-born adults are less likely to use career guidance than their counterparts, and these gaps are particularly large in Australia. For instance, 74% of high-educated mid-career adults use career guidance compared to only 44% of low-educated mid-career adults, the largest gap among participating countries.

Introduction

Career guidance supports adults in navigating career and training opportunities, and is of crucial importance in the current context of rapidly changing skills needs and job transitions arising from the pandemic. This report explores what constitutes high quality career guidance for mid-career adults, as distinct from younger adults and those nearing retirement. Mid-career individuals – adults who have been in the labour market for at least 10 years and have at least 10 years before retirement – could benefit from the support of a career professional in navigating the changing labour market and identifying suitable retraining and upskilling opportunities to remain productive and satisfied at work. This is a group heavily affected by the changes in the labour market: their skills are more likely to become obsolete because they are further away than youth from initial education; yet they still have a significant portion of their work life ahead of them, making significant reskilling both possible and rewarding.

This chapter first examines labour market trends and the effects of the pandemic, and how these are having an impact on the demand and supply of skills. The chapter considers the degree to which mid-career adults are adapting to changes in skill demands by retraining or changing jobs. It concludes that career guidance for mid-career adults could better support them in facilitating employment transitions and finding suitable training opportunities, given the pace of ongoing labour market changes.

The analysis in this report is based on a combination of desk research, video calls with stakeholders in Australia and new evidence from the OECD Survey of Career Guidance for Adults (SCGA). The virtual interviews were conducted with stakeholders at federal and state levels, as well as with private actors and researchers involved in career guidance for adults in Australia. The SCGA is an online survey that sheds light on the use, provision, inclusiveness, and quality of adult career guidance services across countries. In doing so, it fills an important information gap by creating an internationally comparable source of data on the use of adult career guidance services. Already implemented in 10 other countries (Argentina, Brazil, Canada, Chile, France, Germany, Italy, Mexico, New Zealand, and the United States), this survey was conducted in Australia in July and August 2021.

Box 1.1. What is career guidance for adults?

Consistent with the definition used in the OECD Survey of Career Guidance for Adults, this report defines career guidance for adults as "a set of services (public or private) intended to assist adults to make educational, training and occupational choices."

Career guidance for adults can be distinguished from career guidance for young people in schools in various ways. First, adults generally acquire skills through work experiences that are not formally validated. Effective career guidance for adults supports them in identifying employment and training opportunities that leverage these existing skills. Second, career guidance for adults is ideally sensitive to their more complex needs, including family, childcare and financial responsibilities. Third, having been out of school for longer periods, adults are generally less aware of training opportunities and more familiar with the labour market than young people. Effective career guidance considers these factors.

Career guidance differs from job matching services. Job matching is typically reserved for unemployed people where the goal is to place jobseekers into employment. Though career guidance can help jobseekers to find jobs, it ideally takes a more holistic approach where skills, knowledge and abilities are thoroughly assessed, and the individual's constraints and motivations are taken into account when designing career development plans. Also, the metric for success differs for job matching and career guidance. In general, job matching is considered a success if a jobseeker secures employment. Career guidance is considered a success, by contrast, if an individual obtains any number of milestones towards greater employability and personal well-being: acquiring new skills to manage their career,

---

feeling more positively about their labour market prospects, identifying and/or enrolling in a relevant training opportunity, or acquiring sustainable employment in an occupation they enjoy. For the most part, federally funded employment service providers (jobactive) in Australia do not provide career guidance but rather job matching services. However, career guidance is provided through some state-funded employment service providers.

Career guidance for adults has the potential to strengthen skill development, facilitate labour market transitions and support a better match between the supply and demand of skills and labour. Adults have varying levels of knowledge about labour markets and training opportunities, as well as varying abilities to plan their futures. Career guidance has the potential to level these inequalities and support the labour market inclusion of under-represented groups.

This report will use the general term "career guidance advisor" to refer to professionals who provide career guidance. In Australia, advisors working in career guidance can be called "professional career development practitioners" if they have completed a post-graduate career development qualification and/or registered through the Career Industry Council of Australia (CICA).

Source: OECD (2004[1]) *Career Guidance and Public Policy: Bridging The Gap*, https://dx.doi.org/10.1787/9789264105669-en; OECD (2021[2]), *Career Guidance for Adults in a Changing World of Work*, https://doi.org/10.1787/9a94bfad-en.

1.1. A changing labour market context

The COVID-19 pandemic, along with pre-existing trends such as digitalisation, globalisation, population ageing and plans to reach zero-carbon emissions by 2050 ("the green transition"), are changing the Australian labour market. This section discusses these changes and how they affect the demand for skills in the labour market. This is of particular relevance for Australians in their mid-career, given that the skills they acquired in initial education may have become obsolete, and they may require reskilling to remain employable in the changing labour market.

1.1.1. The Australian labour market is making a strong recovery from the pandemic

By Q3 2021, Australia had made a strong recovery from the COVID-19 pandemic, with the unemployment rate below pre-pandemic levels and the employment-to-population ratio above pre-pandemic levels. The initial effect of the pandemic on unemployment was sharp, peaking at 7.4% in July 2020 (Figure 1.1). The increase in unemployment could have been much higher if there had not been a drop in labour force participation and introduction of subsidies for businesses significantly affected by COVID-19 (National Skills Commission, 2021[3]). The easing of restrictions led to an improvement in the labour market, and by February 2022 the unemployment rate had fallen back to 4.3%, even below pre-pandemic levels. The employment-to-population ratio in February 2022 was at 77.2%, 2.7 percentage points higher than the pre-pandemic level (74.5% in March 2020). Mid-career adults, like other age groups, experienced an increase in unemployment during the first year of the pandemic, but unemployment has since recovered and now sits below pre-pandemic levels (Figure 1.2).

Australia's labour market is now tighter than it was prior to COVID-19. Tightness can be seen by a sharp rise in the vacancy-to-unemployment ratio in Australia, as well as in other English-speaking countries (Canada, United Kingdom and the United States) (Romain A Duval et al., 2022[4]). The rise in labour market tightness may be partly due to a change in worker preferences, particularly away from some low-pay jobs. Sectoral job mismatch may also play a role.

Figure 1.1. Employment and unemployment rates have returned to pre-pandemic levels in Australia

Quarterly employment and unemployment rates in Australia for ages 15-64, 2017-21

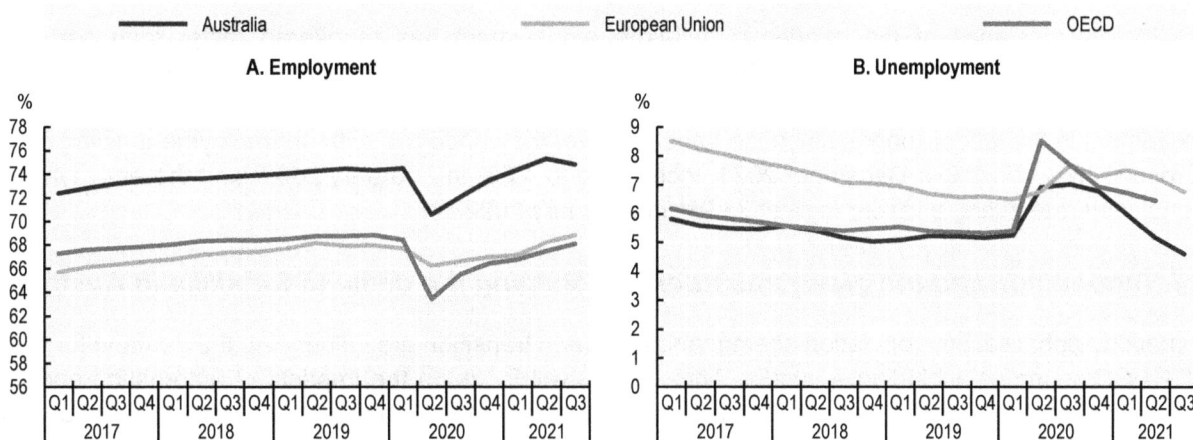

Note: The employment rate is defined as the employed population as a percentage of the working age population. The unemployment rate is defined as the unemployed population as a percentage of the labour force (active population).
Source: OECD (2021[5]), Employment rate (indicator) https://doi.org/10.1787/1de68a9b-en. OECD ((2021[6]), Unemployment rate (indicator). https://doi.org/10.1787/52570002-en (Accessed on 15 January 2022).

Figure 1.2. Average unemployment rate, by age group

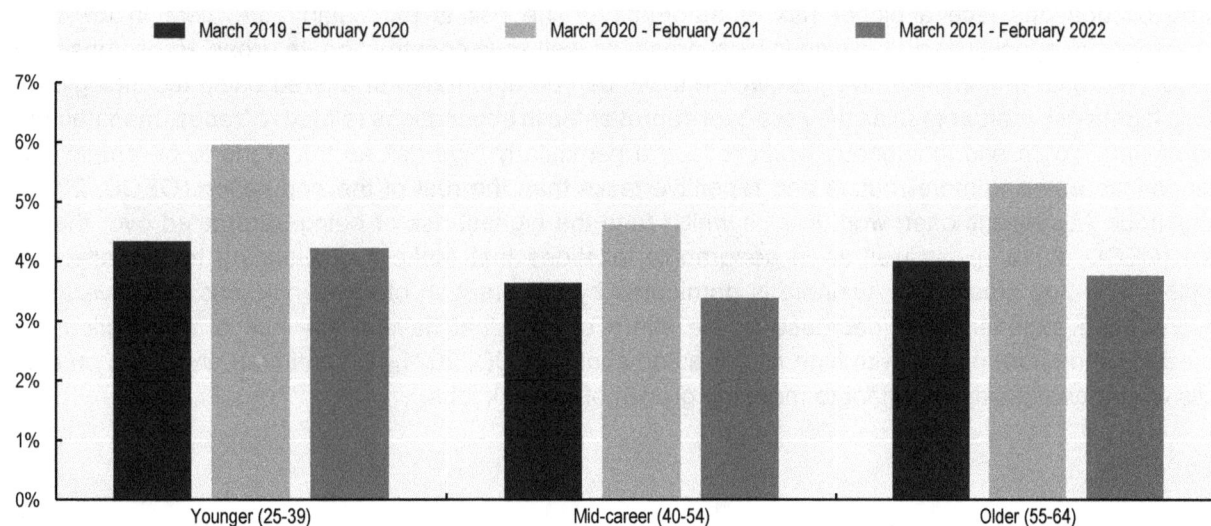

Note: The unemployment rate is defined as the unemployed population as a percentage of the labour force (active population).
Source: Australian Bureau of Statistics https://www.abs.gov.au/statistics/labour/employment-and-unemployment/labour-force-australia-detailed/latest-release.

Some socio-economic groups were hit harder than others in the early stages of the pandemic. Part-time employment decreased more than full-time employment, reflecting wide use of part-time and temporary contracts in the exposed industries. Women were disproportionally affected by the pandemic due to a combination of reasons. Women are overrepresented in service industries that were forced to shut down, they are more likely to be in part-time employment and thus among the first to be considered for retrenchments, and during school lockdown women took on more caring roles in the household, leading to a reduction in working hours. OECD analysis of online vacancy data also shows that there was a larger drop in vacancies and new hires among low-skilled adults versus higher-skilled adults in Australia during the pandemic (OECD, 2021[7]), as well as a substantially lower employment growth for low-wage workers compared to high-wage workers (OECD, 2021[8]).

Since the initial stages of the pandemic, full-time employment has recovered faster than part-time employment. Full-time employment in February 2022 is 4.0% above the level recorded in February 2020, while part-time employment is 0.3% below the February 2020 level. Women have experienced a significant improvement in the labour market since the latest wave of the pandemic, with unemployment hitting close to a record lows of 4.0% in December 2021, inching up to 4.3% in February 2022, and the employment-to-population rate hitting a record high of 73.9% in February 2022.

1.1.2. Automation and the green transition are shaping the demand for skills in Australia

Automation, globalisation, population ageing, and the green transition are influencing the demand for skills in all OECD countries, including Australia. This section will focus on the impacts of automation and the shift to a green economy on the Australian labour market, before moving to a discussion about how Australians in mid-career are adapting to such changes.

The COVID-19 pandemic has accelerated pre-existing trends towards automation, as firm adoption of new technology has increased in response to the pandemic. Australian adults face a lower risk of losing their jobs to automation than on average across the OECD (Figure 1.3). According to OECD estimates prior to the pandemic, 11% of jobs in Australia are at high risk of automation while an additional 25% are at significant risk of change as many tasks could be automated. As jobs become more automated, higher-level skills like digital skills become more in demand.

Some occupations face a higher risk of automation. The risk is particularly prevalent in low-skilled occupations in agriculture and mining in rural areas, as well as in construction. In urban areas, jobs at risk are concentrated in administrative jobs where tasks can be automated or altered using technology. Men face a higher risk than women as they are over-represented in occupations related to trades, manufacturing and mining. Youth and Indigenous workers face a particularly high risk as they tend to be employed in occupations entailing more routine and repetitive tasks than the rest of the population (OECD, 2021[9]). Indigenous Australians often work in jobs which face the highest risk of being automated over the long term (OECD, 2019[10]), as well as in geographic locations that make it challenging to find alternative employment. Job creation in Australia is dominated by the creation of lower-risk jobs. However, some regions have experienced a decrease in the share of jobs that have a low risk of automation, thus increasing the share of jobs with high risk of automation (OECD, 2021[9]). Continued emphasis on digital skills will be particularly important to meet the growth of low-risk jobs.

Figure 1.3. Jobs at risk of automation or significant change

Share of jobs at risk of automation or significant change

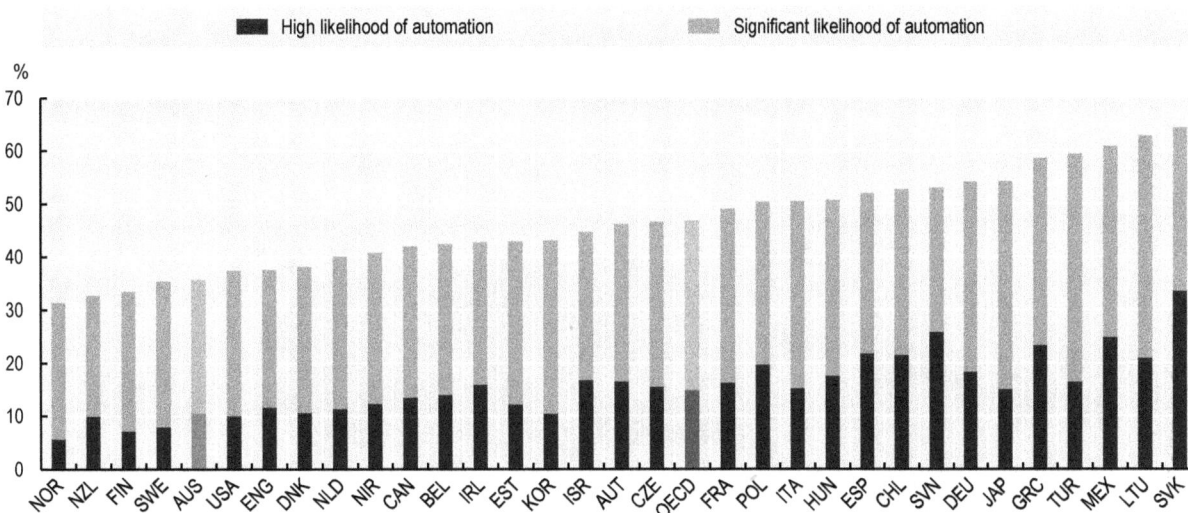

Note: Jobs are at high risk of automation if the likelihood of their job being automated is at least 70%. Jobs at risk of significant change are those with the likelihood of their job being automated estimated at between 50 and 70%. Data for Belgium correspond to Flanders.
Source: OECD calculations based on the Survey of Adult Skills (PIAAC, 2012); and Nedelkoska and Quintini (2018[11]) "Automation, skills use and training", https://doi.org/10.1787/2e2f4eea-en.

The green transition is becoming more pressing as the effects of climate change become more evident, particularly after the 2019-20 Australian bushfire season which caused significant social, financial and ecological losses. The government has recently announced plans of delivering net zero emissions by 2050 (The Australian Government, 2021[12]). The green transition will be accompanied by significant employment opportunities, and estimates show job creation is likely to be concentrated in medium-skilled occupations (ILO, 2019[13]). Already, Australia faces its highest skill shortages in medium-skilled occupations (Figure 1.4). New jobs will be created as part of the green transition, but might not be located in the same industries in which jobs are lost. At the same time, current training systems are not sufficiently aligned with the shifts that are taking place (ILO, 2018[14]). A strong and agile education and training system that is responsive to industry will be necessary to facilitate job transition from declining industries into new, green jobs. Career guidance and training will be crucial to support those who do not have easily transferrable skills.

According to the OECD Skills for Jobs database, which currently refers to 2016 for Australia, Australia displays substantial shortages in medium-skilled occupations and high-skilled occupations. Nearly half of shortages are in high-skilled occupations in Australia (49%), compared with the OECD average of 55%. (Figure 1.4). There are comparatively more shortages in medium-skilled occupations in Australia (51% versus 39% across OECD countries). This presents an opportunity to facilitate transitions of low-skilled workers into medium-skilled occupations. Still, it requires a strong system for identifying people in low-skilled occupations and mapping their training needs to transition into medium-skilled occupations. Career guidance can be a key policy lever in this effort.

Figure 1.4. Australia displays substantial shortages in medium- and high-skilled occupations

Share of employment in occupations in shortage by skill level, 2016

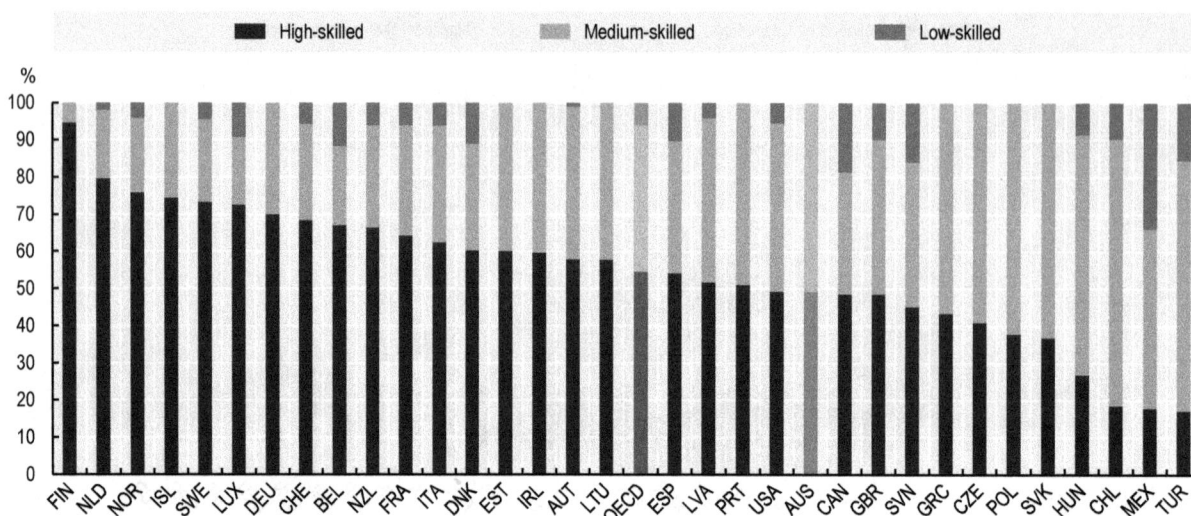

Note: The Skills for Jobs database defines skills as either in shortage or in surplus. These imbalances are measured following a two-step approach. First, an "occupational shortage indicator" is calculated for 33 occupations, based on the analysis of the wage growth, employment growth, hours worked growth, unemployment rate and the change in under-qualification. For each country, long-run trends are compared to the economy-wide trend. Based on the O*NET database, the "occupational shortage indicator" is then used to build indicators of skills shortages and surpluses. High, medium and low-skilled occupations are defined based on the following ISCO codes: high (ISCO 1-3), medium (ISCO 4-8) and low (ISCO 9). Shares of employment in each skill tier are computed as the corresponding employment in each group over the total number of workers in shortage in each country. Data refer to the latest year for which information is available.
Source: OECD Skills for Jobs database, oecdskillsforjobsdatabase.org, accessed 15 December 2021.

1.2. Mid-career adults are an important target group for training and guidance

In the current context of changing demand for skills, mid-career adults are an important target group for training and guidance. This section discusses the characteristics of mid-career adults, why they can benefit from career guidance, and what type of training and guidance can be most beneficial for them.

1.2.1. Characterising mid-career adults

While there is no commonly accepted age range that corresponds to mid-career adults, adults in this group have generally participated in the labour market long enough to have acquired skills through both education and work experience, but are still relatively far away from retirement. This report defines mid-career adults as individuals with at least 10 years of labour market experience and who have at least 10 years before retirement. Any data analysis in the report that refers to the mid-career adult population will approximate this group by focusing on the sample of adults aged 40-54 (regardless of their years of labour market experience and years to retirement).

Focusing on mid-career adults supports the policy goal of encouraging Australians to be lifelong learners. As mid-career adults have participated in the workforce for a substantial period of time, they have acquired skills and experience. At the same time, the skills they acquired in initial education may have become obsolete or may no longer be relevant for the work they are doing. With many years left before retirement, mid-career adults still have a significant portion of their work life ahead of them. They may thus need help to build on their existing skills to progress, but they have time to enjoy a return on their training investment before they retire.

1.2.2. Mid-career adults have particular training and guidance needs

Data from the 2012 OECD Survey of Adult Skills (Programme for the International Assessment of Adult Competencies – PIAAC) show that mid-career adults participate less in job-related training than younger adults (Figure 1.5). According to the survey, 56% of mid-career adults participated in formal or non-formal job-related training over a 12-month period compared to 62% of younger adults. Generally, mid-career adults train less than young adults, partly because the opportunity cost of training is higher due to their income being higher. Mid-career adults are more often in full-time employment, and inflexibility in the work schedule can lead to less training. Other factors that result in less training among mid-career adults are less awareness of both the existence of training programmes and their benefits given that for most of them a long time has passed since they were in initial education, and more family responsibilities which limit the time they have available to train.

Figure 1.5. Participation in formal or non-formal job-related training, adults aged 25-64, 2012/2015

Share of adults aged 25-64 who participated in formal or non-formal job-related training over the previous 12 months, by country

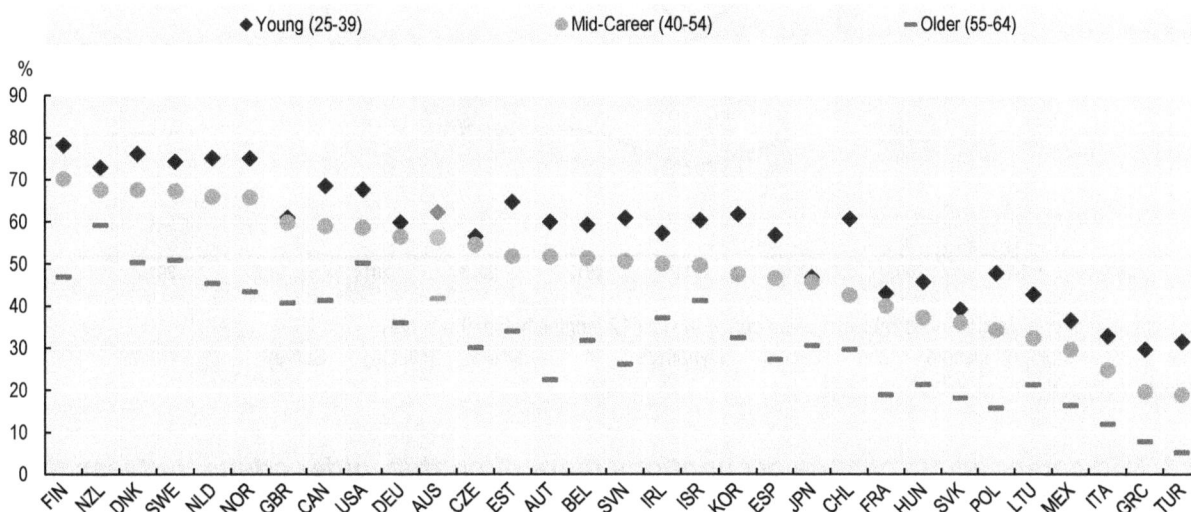

Note: Data refer to 2012 for most countries, except Chile, Greece, Lithuania, New Zealand, Slovenia and Turkey where they refer to 2015.
Source: *OECD Survey of Adult Skills* (PIAAC), https://www.oecd.org/skills/piaac/data/.

National data shows that there has been a small decrease in job-related training among mid-career adults in Australia (OECD, 2019[15]). The Household, Income and Labour Dynamics in Australia (HILDA) survey indicates a slight decline in job-related training for mid-career adults between 2007 and 2017, with 27% of mid-career adults participating in training in 2017 compared to 29% in 2007 (Figure 1.6). Further, the number of days attending a training course has declined for mid-career adults (from 7.9 days in 2007 to 6.3 days in 2017). However, over the same time period there was an increase in number of training courses attended (from 3.7 to 4.2 courses). This indicates that mid-career adults are attending more courses but of shorter duration, either because the courses are more efficient, less substantive, or so that they fit in better with family and work responsibilities.

Mid-career adults' motives for training are focused on improving current employment rather than preparing for a potential change in occupation. According to the HILDA survey, the most common motivation for training is to improve conditions in one's current employment, either by improving skills in one's current job (15%) or maintaining professional status and/or meeting occupation requirements (13%). Only 5% of respondents trained to prepare for a job they might do in the future. Other reasons cited for training were to develop skills generally (12%), health and safety concerns (6%) or to help get started in the job (2%).

Figure 1.6. Participation in job-related training in the past 12 months, 2007-17

Share of adults aged 25-64 who participated in any job-related training over the previous 12 months, by age group

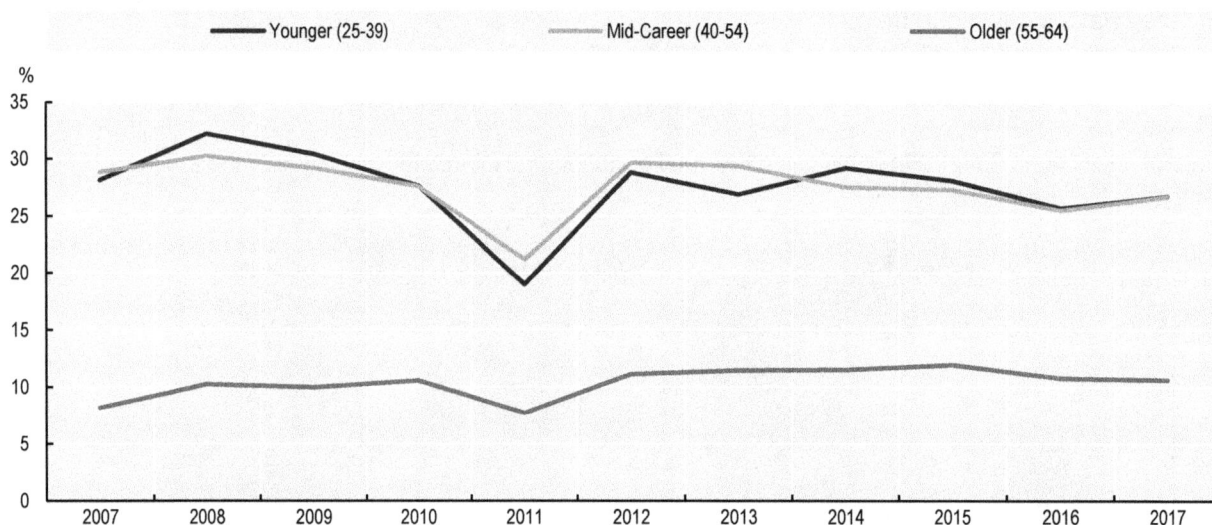

Note: Data refer to participation in job-related training during the last 12 months before the survey.
Source: Household, Income and Labour Dynamics in Australia (HILDA) Survey – Waves 2001-2017, https://melbourneinstitute.unimelb.edu.au/hilda.

1.2.3. Mid-career adults change occupations more often than older adults, but less than younger adults

The rate at which adults change occupation declines with age. In Australia, 19% of mid-career adults changed occupation between 2016 and 2017 (Figure 1.7). This is lower than the rate for younger adults (23%), but higher than the rate for older adults (12%). Figure 1.7 shows a slight decline in job transition rates for all age groups since 2001/02, when 23% of mid-career adults changed occupation. As one might expect, mid-career adults in occupations with a high risk of automation change occupation more often than those in lower-risk occupations (Figure 1.8). They may switch jobs more often either because their role becomes obsolete or due to less stable working conditions in high-risk jobs that result in transitions from one high-risk job to another. At the same time, adults in high-risk jobs also train less than those in low-risk jobs (Figure 1.8). This is concerning, as people in high-risk occupations should ideally be training more to enable their transition to more stable employment.

Figure 1.7. Annual occupation transition rate, 2001-17

Percentage of adults who changed occupation, by year and by age group

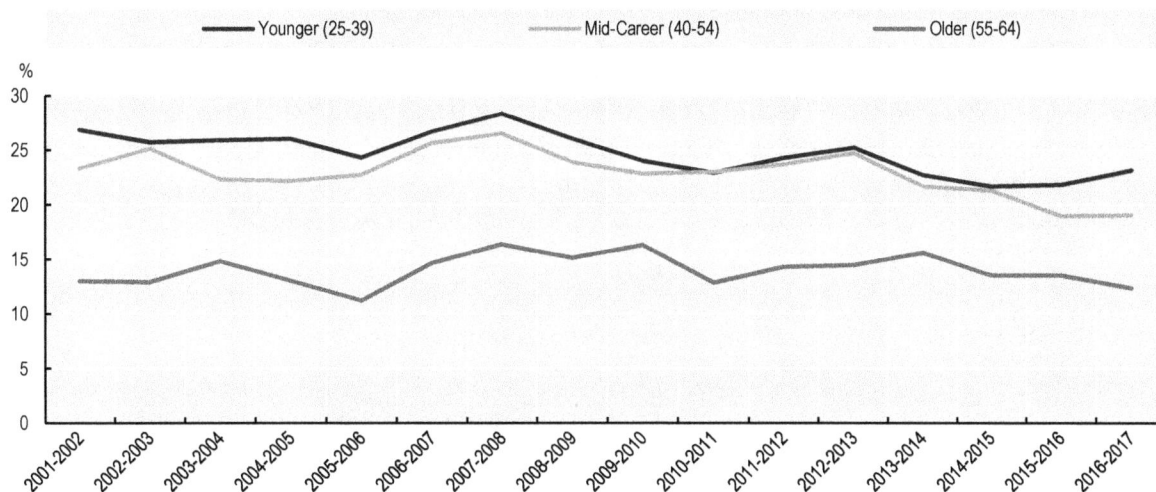

Note: The calculations are based on the two-digit occupations of the Australian and New Zealand Standard Classification of Occupations (ANZSCO).
Source: Household, Income and Labour Dynamics in Australia (HILDA) Survey – Waves 2001-2017, https://melbourneinstitute.unimelb.edu.au/hilda.

Figure 1.8. Rates of occupation changes and training in Australia, by occupation and risk of automation

Shares of mid-career adults who changed occupation between 2016-17 and who participated in work-related training in 2017, by one-digit ANZCO occupation code and risk of automation

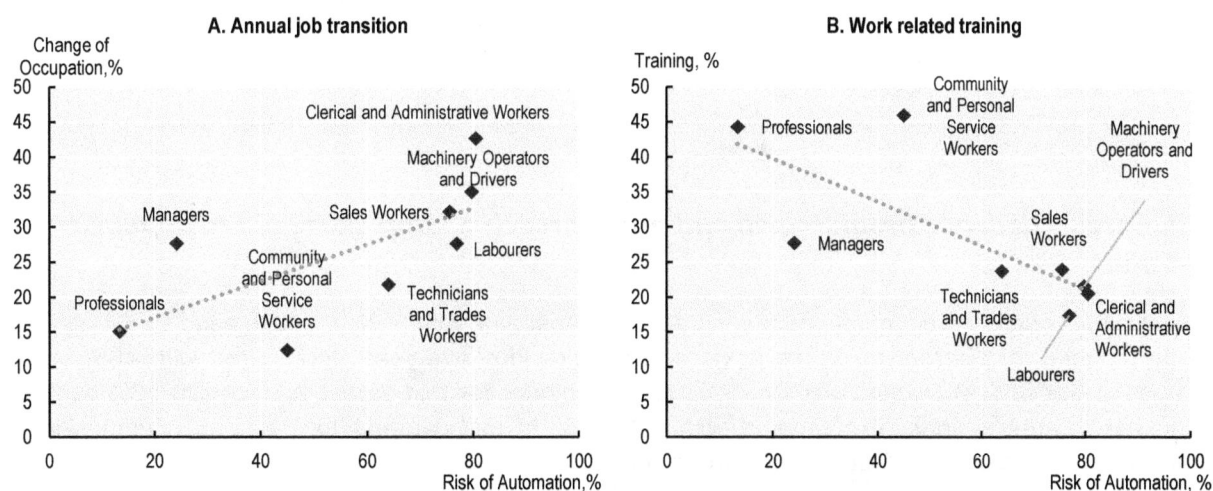

Note: The annual job transition calculations are based on the one-digit occupation code from the Australian and New Zealand Standard Classification of Occupations (ANZSCO). The occupations shown in Panel A represent the initial occupation in 2016.
Source: Household, Income and Labour Dynamics in Australia (HILDA) Survey – Wave 2016-2017, https://melbourneinstitute.unimelb.edu.au/hilda.

1.3. Use of career guidance by mid-career adults

Career guidance plays a vital role in enabling adults to participate in training. It assists individuals in assessing their training needs and in making well-informed educational, training and occupational choices (Box 1.1). Across OECD countries, policy on career guidance has tended to focus on young people in schools, who are about to transition either into higher levels of education or into the labour market. There is growing attention, however, given to adult skills and training and how career guidance can support adults in adapting to changing demand for skills. As noted above, adults in mid-career are particularly well-placed to benefit from career guidance services. This section reviews the use of career guidance by mid-career adults in Australia, based on the OECD Survey of Career Guidance for Adults (SCGA).

Box 1.2. OECD Survey of Career Guidance for Adults

This report uses data collected in the OECD 2020/2021 Survey of Career Guidance for Adults (SCGA). The SCGA was conducted to better understand adults' experience with career guidance services and to improve international data on its use, coverage and inclusiveness. It currently covers 11 countries: Argentina, Australia, Brazil, Canada, Chile, France, Germany, Italy, Mexico, New Zealand and the United States.

Data collection for Australia was conducted between end-July and mid-August 2021. The survey was disseminated online to a panel of individuals aged 25-64. A stratified sample methodology imposed quotas to have a representative sample of the country's population in terms of age, gender and region.[1] The final Australian sample size after quality checks was 2 999 observations, of which 1 110 were mid-career adults (age 40-54). Education weights are applied using OECD data (2020[16]) to facilitate cross-country comparison. For a full description of the methodology, see OECD (2022[17]; 2021[2]).

The online survey was conducted in different countries over 2020 and 2021, at different stages of the COVID-19 pandemic. Cross-country differences in the reported use of career services may therefore partially reflect measures to address the employment effects of the pandemic.

Source: OECD (2022[17]), *Career Guidance for Adults in Canada*, https://doi.org/10.1787/0e596882-en; OECD (2021[2]), *Career Guidance for Adults in a Changing World of Work*, https://dx.doi.org/10.1787/9a94bfad-en; OECD, (2020[16]), *Education at a Glance 2020: OECD Indicators*, https://dx.doi.org/10.1787/69096873-en.

1.3.1. Career guidance programmes and portals reach a large share of the population in Australia

There is a high use of career guidance among adults in Australia, with 51% of adults aged 25-64 reporting that they spoke to a career guidance advisor in the previous five years (compared with 40% among countries in the SCGA) (Figure 1.9). The rate is even higher for mid-career adults, with 56% reporting having used career guidance (compared with only 38% of mid-career adults among countries in the SCGA). However, a couple of caveats are worth noting.

First, many respondents will have received job matching services rather than career guidance. As elaborated in Chapter 2, a large share of adults (24%) and mid-career adults (24%) report receiving career guidance from publicly funded employment services[2] (whether federally funded or state-funded) in Australia. There is no federally funded employment service that offers career guidance in Australia, though some state-level and state-funded employment services do offer career guidance (e.g. Victoria). Job matching is a part of Australia's federally funded programme for jobseekers receiving welfare payments, and the service is carried out by private job service providers (jobactive networks). It is therefore likely that respondents who report having received career guidance from a federally funded employment services in Australia actually received job matching services.

Second, the share of adults who have used career guidance reflects not only those who have received career guidance through traditional modes (i.e. face-to-face delivery with a career guidance advisor), but also those who interacted with a career guidance advisor by phone, through online chat, video conferencing, and through instant messaging. As the Australian survey was conducted later in the COVID-19 pandemic relative to other countries in the survey, the high use may partially reflect a greater use of online career guidance as well as greater availability of public programs to respond to the employment effects of the pandemic.

Figure 1.9. Use of career guidance services among adults

Share of mid-career adults who spoke with a career guidance advisor over the past five years, by country

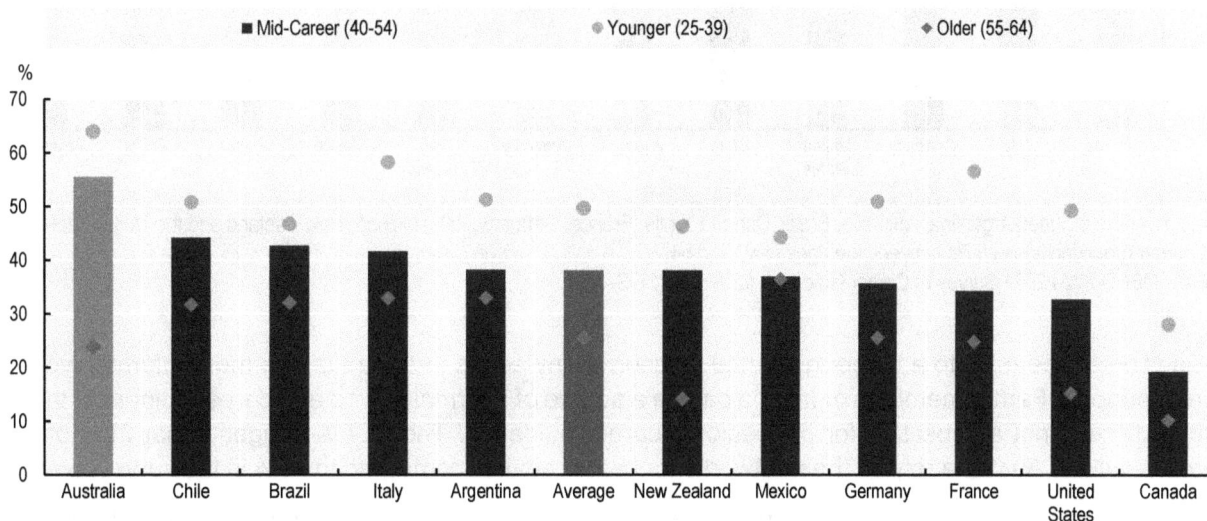

Note: Average includes Argentina, Australia, Brazil, Canada, Chile, France, Germany, Italy, Mexico, New Zealand and the United States. Data refers to the last time the respondent spoke to a career guidance advisor.
Source: OECD 2020/2021 Survey of Career Guidance for Adults (SCGA).

The intensity of service, i.e. the number of interactions that an adult has with a career guidance advisor every year, is another important indicator of how well career guidance services are used. It provides insights on whether there is a follow-up after a first consultation, and if there is a continuity in the service delivery. Most mid-career adults who use career guidance services in Australia have multiple interactions with advisors. Less than a quarter of mid-career adults who spoke with a career guidance advisor over the past year had a single interaction (23%), while 40% had two interactions, and 37% spoke with a career guidance advisor three or more times (compared with 24%, 38%, and 38% across the average for other countries in the survey, respectively) (Figure 1.10). Repeated interactions with career guidance advisors may indicate an execution of a more long-term guidance plan and follow-up. Jobseekers receiving support through jobactive also typically have obligations to attend ongoing appointments.

Figure 1.10. Intensity of use of career guidance services among mid-career adults

Share of mid-career adults who spoke with a career guidance advisor over the past five years, by number of interactions

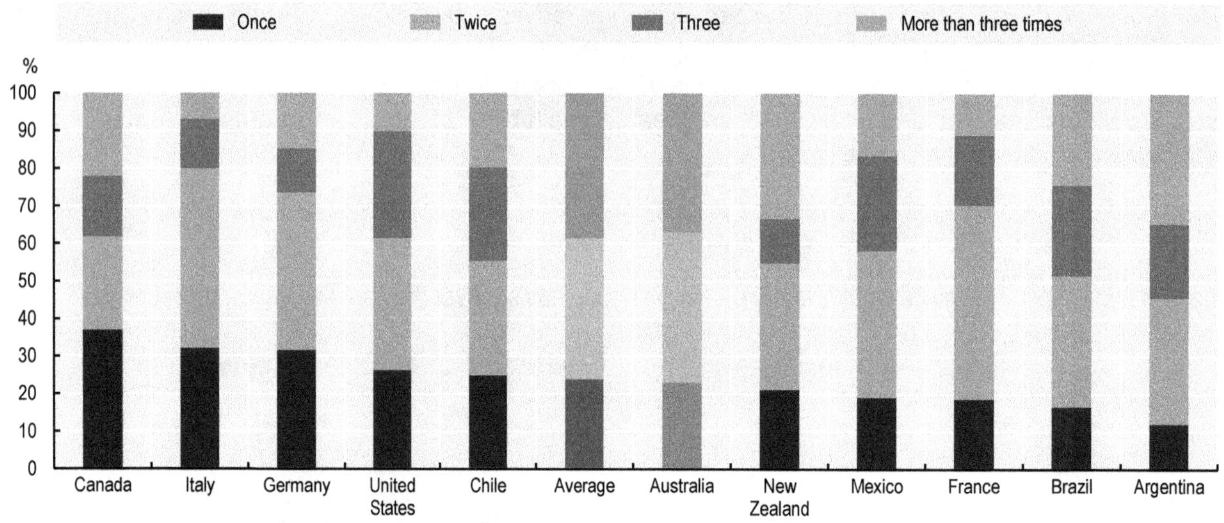

Notes: Average includes Argentina, Australia, Brazil, Canada, Chile, France, Germany, Italy, Mexico, New Zealand and the United States. The mid-career group includes adults between the ages of 40 and 54.
Source: OECD 2020/2021 Survey of Career Guidance for Adults (SCGA).

In addition to speaking to a career guidance advisor, many adults in Australia use more informal types of career support. Family members or friends can be a source of informal advice and career guidance, though such advice is not a substitute for professional career guidance. The SCGA suggests that 29% of mid-career adults in Australia rely on their networks for career advice, compared to 25% in the survey average.

Mid-career adults are more likely to participate in informal career development activities than either younger or older adults. Participating in career development activities allows mid-career adults to gain better understanding of employment and training opportunities available to them, giving them an opportunity to think more concretely about their skills, ambitions, and career preferences. More than half of mid-career adults (62%) participated in one or more career development activities in the 12 months preceding the survey, reasonably more than the survey average of 51% (Figure 1.11). The most common activities were visiting a training provider (27%), speaking with one's manager or HR professionals at work (23%), participating in a job rotation/work site visit (17%) or visiting a job fair (15%). Only 5% of mid-career adults did an internship, apprenticeship or traineeship. Such activities are slightly more common among younger adults (8%).

Figure 1.11. Participation in career development activities

Share of adults who participated in other types of career development over the past year, by activity and age group

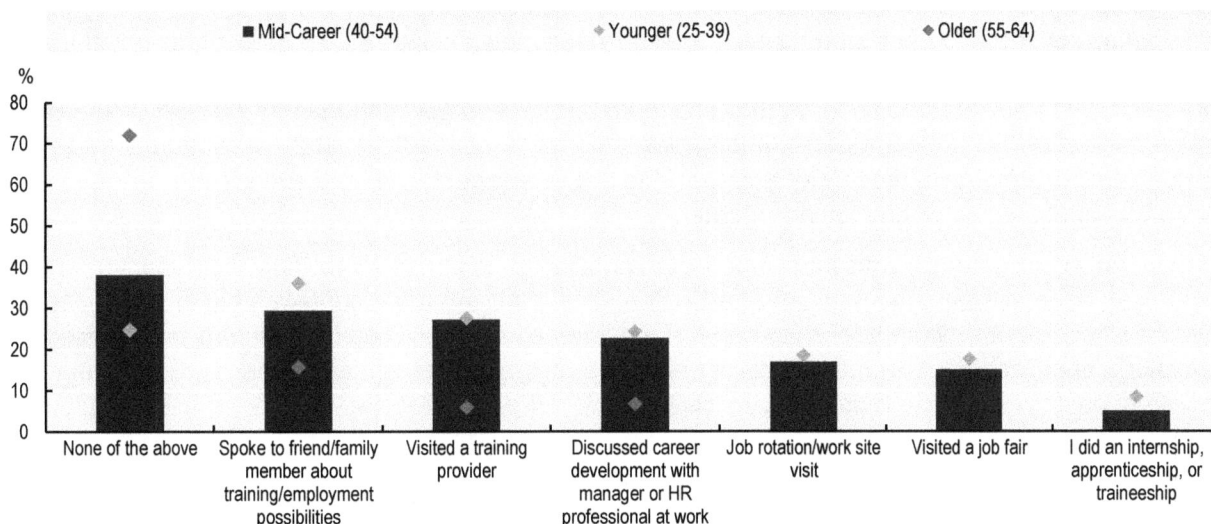

Note: Respondents could choose more than one answer. The value for older adults was suppressed for some of the activities due to low sample size of the sub-group (job rotation/work site visit, visited a job fair, did an internship/apprenticeship/traineeship).
Source: OECD 2020/2021 Survey of Career Guidance for Adults (SCGA).

1.3.2. Use of career guidance among mid-career adults in Australia is unequal

Compared with other countries in the survey, use of career guidance among adults is more unequal in Australia. Figure 1.12 shows the gaps in use of career guidance in Australia by different groups, and these gaps are relatively large in international comparison.

Figure 1.12. Use of career guidance service, by socio-economic and demographic characteristics

Share of all adults aged 25-64 who spoke to a career guidance advisor over the past five years, by group

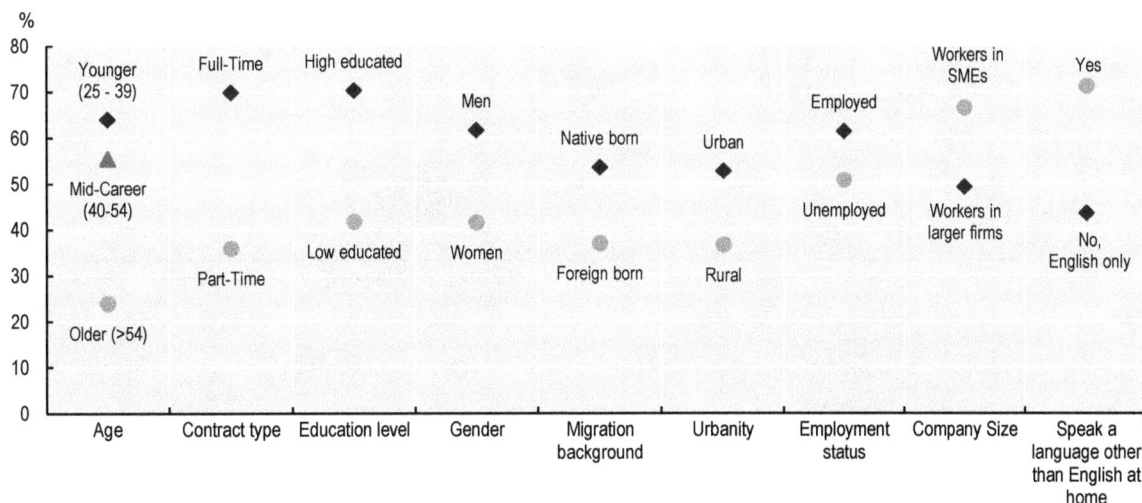

Note. The low educated group includes adults with a low or medium level of education (i.e. less than a bachelor's degree).
Source: OECD 2020/2021 Survey of Career Guidance for Adults (SCGA).

Focusing on mid-career adults, these gaps are even more pronounced (Figure 1.13). Adults in part-time employment use career guidance much less than those in full-time employment (45 percentage points). Low-educated adults use career guidance less than high-educated adults, and this gap is much higher than the survey average (30 percentage points vs. 14 percentage points) and is the highest among all participating countries. Other important gaps exist between men and women (29 percentage points), adults living in rural areas and those living in urban areas (27 percentage points), and native-born and foreign-born adults (21 percentage points). Higher usage among mid-career men than mid-career women could be a reflection of their different personal and professional responsibilities. Mid-career adults have more family obligations that take time away from seeking out career guidance, and such family obligations are unequally distributed between men and women.

By contrast, other potentially disadvantaged groups take up guidance more than their counterparts do, such as workers in small and medium-sized enterprises (SMEs) (15 percentage points) and those who speak a language other than English at home (30 percentage points). The latter finding could reflect that Australia's labour market integration programmes for skilled migrants contain career support or that non-English speaking adults are more likely to be unemployed and to receive assistance from employment services.

Higher inequality in the use of career guidance in Australia is worrying because it means that career guidance is not reaching those who most need it. Socio-economic inequalities become increasingly challenging to address the longer they persist. Reaching out to under-represented groups to connect them with career guidance services could improve training participation rates and labour market outcomes for these groups.

Figure 1.13. Use of career guidance service by mid-career adults, by socio-economic and demographic characteristics

Share of mid-career adults who spoke to a career guidance advisor over the past five years, by group

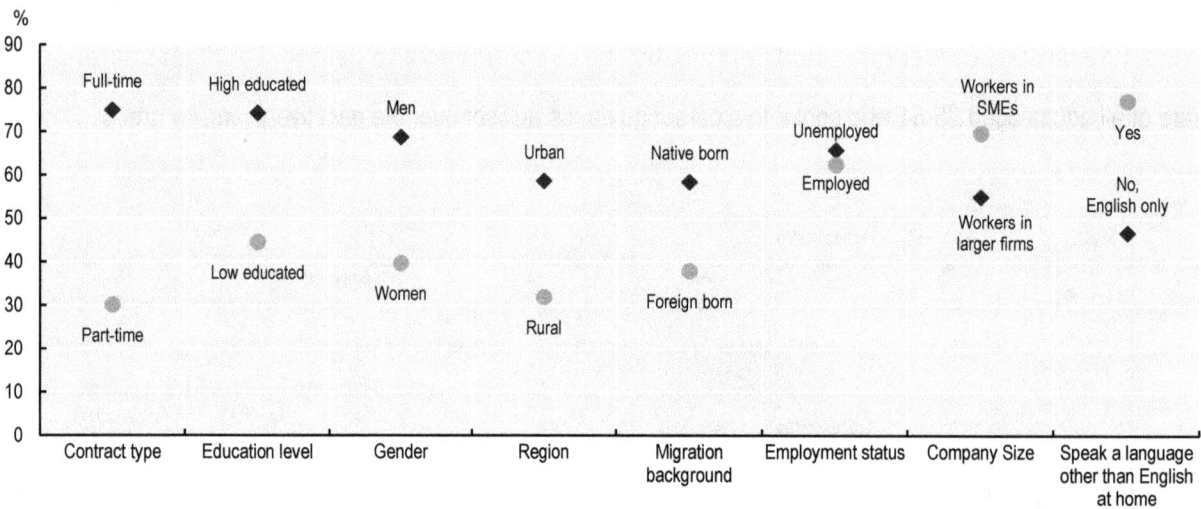

Note: The low educated group includes adults with a low or medium level of education (i.e. less than a bachelor's degree). The mid-career group includes adults between the ages of 40 and 54.
Source: OECD 2020/2021 Survey of Career Guidance for Adults (SCGA).

References

ILO (2019), "Skills for a Greener Future: A Global View", http://www.ilo.org/publns. (accessed on 14 December 2021). [13]

ILO (2018), "Skills for Green Jobs in Australia", http://www.ilo.org/publns. (accessed on 19 January 2022). [14]

National Skills Commission (2021), *Australian Jobs Report*, https://www.nationalskillscommission.gov.au/australian-jobs-report (accessed on 18 November 2021). [3]

Nedelkoska, L. and G. Quintini (2018), "Automation, skills use and training", *OECD Social, Employment and Migration Working Papers*, No. 202, OECD Publishing, Paris, https://doi.org/10.1787/2e2f4eea-en. [11]

OECD (2022), *Career Guidance for Adults in Canada*, Getting Skills Right, OECD Publishing, Paris, https://doi.org/10.1787/0e596882-en. [17]

OECD (2021), "An assessment of the impact of COVID-19 on job and skills demand using online job vacancy data", *OECD Policy Responses to Coronavirus (COVID-19)*, OECD Publishing, Paris, https://doi.org/10.1787/20fff09e-en. [7]

OECD (2021), *Career Guidance for Adults in a Changing World of Work*, Getting Skills Right, OECD Publishing, Paris, https://doi.org/10.1787/9a94bfad-en. [2]

OECD (2022), *Employment rate* (indicator), https://doi.org/10.1787/1de68a9b-en (accessed on 15 January 2022). [5]

OECD (2021), *OECD Economic Surveys: Australia 2021*, OECD Publishing, Paris, https://doi.org/10.1787/ce96b16a-en. [8]

OECD (2021), *Preparing for the Future of Work Across Australia*, OECD Reviews on Local Job Creation, OECD Publishing, Paris, https://doi.org/10.1787/9e506cad-en. [9]

OECD (2022), *Unemployment rate* (indicator), https://doi.org/10.1787/52570002-en (accessed on 15 January 2022). [6]

OECD (2020), *Education at a Glance 2020: OECD Indicators*, OECD Publishing, Paris, https://doi.org/10.1787/69096873-en. [16]

OECD (2019), *Financial Incentives to Promote Adult Learning in Australia*, Getting Skills Right, OECD Publishing, Paris, https://doi.org/10.1787/c79badcc-en. [15]

OECD (2019), *Indigenous Employment and Skills Strategies in Australia*, OECD Reviews on Local Job Creation, OECD Publishing, Paris, https://doi.org/10.1787/dd1029ea-en. [10]

OECD (2004), *Career Guidance and Public Policy: Bridging the Gap*, OECD Publishing, Paris, https://doi.org/10.1787/9789264105669-en. [1]

Romain A Duval et al. (2022), *Labor Market Tightness in Advanced Economies*, International Monetary Fund, https://www.imf.org/en/Publications/Staff-Discussion-Notes/Issues/2022/03/30/Labor-Market-Tightness-in-Advanced-Economies-515270 (accessed on 15 April 2022). [4]

The Australian Government (2021), "Australia's Long-Term Emissions Reduction Plan", [12]
Department of Industry, Science, Energy and Resources, https://www.industry.gov.au/data-and-publications/australias-long-term-emissions-reduction-plan (accessed on 18 November 2021).

Notes

[1] The age and gender quotas were based on UN World Population Prospects statistics, while the regional quotas were based on Cint's data.

[2] The delivery of publicly funded employment services in Australia are contracted out to private and non-profit providers.

2 What constitutes effective career guidance for mid-career adults?

This chapter elaborates on what constitutes high-quality career guidance for mid-career adults. Taking into account their unique needs, the chapter considers how career guidance services for mid-career adults should be delivered, how to motivate mid-career adults to seek out career guidance, who should provide the services, and how to fund them.

In Brief

Effective career guidance for mid-career adults takes into account their specific needs and challenges

Mid-career adults have specific needs when it comes to career guidance and these should be taken into account when designing career guidance services. The key findings from this chapter are:

- Mid-career adults have acquired skills through informal learning over many years of work experience. A first step in guidance for this group should be to make their skills visible and identify their transferable skills. Only 20% of mid-career adults in Australia reported having their skills assessed via a test. Much more common was to have their skills assessed during an interview (70%).

- Once their skills are assessed, career guidance should outline the gap between the skills that mid-career adults have and those needed to perform their desired role. Clear career and training pathways are needed. The final outcome should be a personalised career development roadmap that outlines the training and career development activities required to achieve their objectives. In Australia, a high share of mid-career adult users of career guidance report having received a personalised career development roadmap (75% relative to 55% in other surveyed countries).

- Mid-career adults report different reasons for not accessing career guidance. In Australia, 56% of mid-career adults reported not needing the service, while 20% did not know such services existed. There is also a time constraint, with 10% of women reporting they did not have time due to family responsibilities (compared to 4% of men), and 13% of men reporting time constraints due to work (compared to 4% of women).

- A high share of mid-career adults in Australia seek career guidance to progress in their current job (43%), for which career guidance provided by their employer or by an employer group is well suited and more frequently used than in other countries (16% and 11%, respectively). As in other countries, publicly funded employment services are a commonly used provider of career services in Australia (24%), though these mainly entail job matching services. Private career guidance providers are used considerably less in Australia than elsewhere (12% versus 23%) despite the potential to support mid-career adults who wish to change job or industry.

- Mid-career adults in Australia are more likely to report paying for career services out-of-pocket than are those in other countries: 57% of mid-career users of career guidance paid out-of-pocket, compared to the country average of 33%. As few adults use privately provided career guidance, it is likely that these users paid for other services that indirectly included a career guidance component, such as training courses. Australia does not offer financial incentives to support co-funding of private career guidance. International examples include career vouchers in Belgium or subsidised career guidance in the Netherlands and France.

Introduction

Chapter 1 highlighted the particular challenges faced by mid-career adults in the labour market. Survey evidence from Australia shows that, compared with younger adults, mid-career adults are less likely to change jobs or to train. Greater family responsibilities than younger adults means that they may be less geographically mobile when it comes to considering potential job opportunities, and have less time for training and career development. For most mid-career adults, it would be many years since they were in initial education, and they would likely be unfamiliar with the education and training system and available training opportunities. Finally, mid-career adults would have acquired skills through work experience that have not been formally validated. Finding ways to make these skills visible will facilitate their job transitions, shorten training pathways and improve the matching of skill supply and demand.

Taking these challenges into account, this chapter elaborates on what constitutes high-quality career guidance for mid-career adults by looking at how career guidance services should be delivered, how to motivate mid-career adults to seek out career guidance, who should provide the services, and how to fund them.

2.1. How should career guidance services be delivered to mid-career adults?

Career guidance services need to be delivered in a way that takes into account the particular challenges and needs of mid-career adults.

An important component of career guidance for mid-career adults is making their skills visible and identifying their transferable skills. Having spent many years in the labour market, mid-career adults have acquired skills through informal learning (i.e. non-institutionalised learning activities that are unstructured and can take place anywhere), including learning by doing and learning from others. Indeed, this type of job-related learning at work is much more common than either non-formal learning (i.e. institutionalised learning activities which are either of short duration or not recognised by the relevant education or equivalent authorities) or training towards a formal qualification (Fialho, Quintini and Vandeweyer, 2019[1]). High-quality career guidance for mid-career adults entails making these informally acquired skills visible. Doing so ensures a better assessment of skills gaps associated with potential employment or training goals, and enables shorter training pathways. As is the case in other countries, the most common method used by career guidance advisors in Australia to assess adults' skills is simply asking about a person's experience and qualifications during an interview (Figure 2.1). Nearly 70% of mid-career adults who used career guidance reported that this is how their skills were assessed. Only 20% of mid-career adults reported completing a test to have their skills assessed. Tests with a skills focus are both less subjective than interviews, and also more likely to capture a more comprehensive picture of what mid-career adults can do, because they place less emphasis on formal qualifications or work experience. Australia has introduced several career guidance programmes for mid-career adults that incorporate psychometric, skills and/or employment testing (Box 2.1) but the scale of these programmes is very limited.

Figure 2.1. Methods for assessing skills

Share of mid-career adults who spoke to a career guidance advisor over the past five years, by age and method for assessing skills

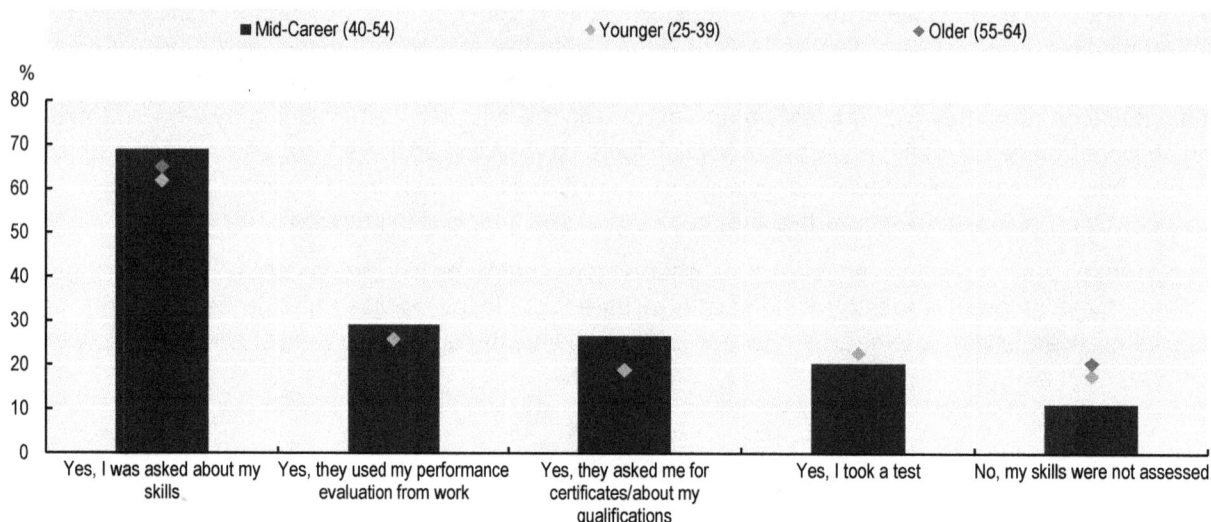

Note: The value for older adults was suppressed in some cases due to insufficient sample size (this applied to use of performance evaluation, asking about certificates/qualifications and taking a test). Respondents could choose more than one answer. Data refers to the last time the respondent spoke to a career guidance advisor.
Source: OECD 2020/2021 Survey of Career Guidance for Adults (SCGA).

Box 2.1. Federal level career guidance programmes for mid-career adults in Australia that emphasise skills assessments and personalised career development roadmaps

Skills Checkpoint for Older Workers

Operating across all Australian states and territories, and administered by the Department of Education, Skills and Employment (DESE), this programme targets Australians aged 40+ who are either recently unemployed or working but at risk of becoming unemployed. To avoid service duplication, only adults who are not registered for assistance through an Australian Government employment services programme, e.g. jobactive or Disability Employment Services, are eligible. The programme provides free, tailored advice and guidance on transitioning into new roles within their current industry or finding pathways to a new career. Participants can receive skills and employment assessment services, career advice and coaching sessions, including development of an individual Career Plan. The programme tests participants' foundation skills, identifies gaps in skills and measures the participants' aptitude for a variety of training pathways and occupations. If the programme identifies a need for training to upskill or reskill, participants may be eligible for support for training costs: up to 75% of costs for occupations in national shortage or 50% of costs for training not related to occupations in shortage (max. AUD 2 200).

On 1 January 2022, the number of places available under the programme was doubled from 5 000 per year to 10 000 per year, though the cap has never been hit. Between December 2018 (when the programme started) and December 2021, 11 630 Australians completed the programme. Around 63% of these participants accessed training funding through the Skills and Training incentive (also administered by DESE). Data is not collected about training starts, completions or employment outcomes related to the programme.

> **Mid-Career Checkpoint**
>
> The Mid-Career Checkpoint programme targets working-age people who have taken time out of the workforce to care for their families and are looking to return to paid employment or advance their careers. The programme is in a pilot phase, operating in New South Wales, Victoria and Queensland, and is delivered as a hybrid model with face-to-face and online sessions. The programme was recently expanded to include support for workers in female-dominated, COVID-19 affected industries. It provides participants with a free skills and employment assessment, tailored career advice and coaching sessions. The programme focuses on matching the participants' employment goals with their skills and qualifications, and where applicable, can measure aptitude through psychometric, skills and/or employment testing.
>
> All participants receive a customised Skills, Training and Employment Plan (STEP) that identifies their attributes, skills and qualifications, as well as any skills gaps and details their employment goals. Each participant's STEP provides information on local employment and training opportunities in line with the participant's employment goals. Where a participant's STEP recommends specific accredited training to upskill or reskill, up to AUD 3 000 is available to support that training. Between July 2020 and December 2021, 363 participants participated in the pilot. Data is not collected about training starts, completions or employment outcomes related to the programme.
>
> Source: Department of Education, Skills and Employment.

The recognition of prior learning (RPL) is a more formal way of assessing and validating an adult's skills. It is particularly useful in supporting upskilling and reskilling pathways of mid-career adults who lack formal qualifications. These processes are often offered by education and training institutions and lead to formal certification of skills acquired outside of formal training. The process involves demonstrating achievement of competencies, often by preparing a portfolio of relevant work or demonstrating one's ability to carry out tasks in practice. Recognition of prior learning can shorten retraining pathways by giving adults credit for skills they already have, and thus accelerating their transition to new jobs or sectors. These processes are often complex and demanding, and guidance that supports adults in these processes of having their skills recognised can be valuable to mid-career adults. Finland's competency-based vocational education and training (VET) programmes are examples of career guidance that supports the adult in completing an RPL process (Box 2.2). Tasmania's Rapid Response Skills Initiative is another example (Box 2.4).

Personalised career development roadmaps are another important component of quality career guidance, particularly for mid-career adults. Such roadmaps spell out the sequence of activities that an adult should take to achieve their employment and/or training objectives. They start from a thorough assessment of the adult's skills, aspirations and background. They can be particularly helpful to support mid-career adults considering job or occupation transitions, by providing a clear action plan for the training and other career development activities they would need to carry out. Use of personalised career development roadmaps is quite high in Australia, with 75% of mid-career adults who used career guidance reporting that they received one (Figure 2.2). This is well above the survey average (55%). Both the Skills Checkpoint and the Mid-Career Checkpoint feature a personalised career development roadmap as a component of their career guidance programmes.

Figure 2.2. Personalised career development roadmap

Share of adults who spoke to a career guidance advisor over the past five years who reported receiving a personalised career development roadmap

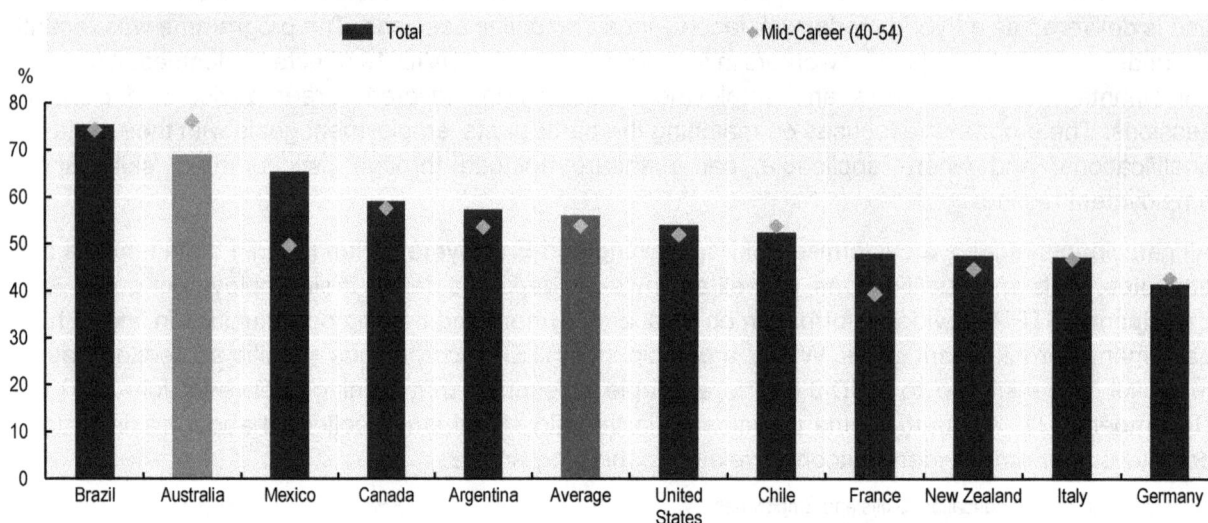

Note: Average includes Argentina, Australia, Brazil, Canada, Chile, France, Germany, Italy, Mexico, New Zealand and the United States. A personalised career development roadmap (also called an individual action plan) is a resource prepared by the advisor based on the user's background and skills. It sets out a planned sequence of activities to help the user towards achieving their education and employment objectives. Total population refers to all adults aged 25 to 64 in the survey.
Source: OECD 2020/2021 Survey of Career Guidance for Adults (SCGA).

Career guidance for mid-career adults should clarify career and training pathways. To support progression within one's firm, workers need to understand which skills are needed to perform the different roles within the firm and employers should make this information transparent. Encouraging the use of mentoring, career conversations with HR professionals, and job rotation within firms can help adults become familiar with the skills required in different roles. In some countries, the government supports the development of career pathways which map the skills and training needed to perform different roles within a given occupation or sector. In Japan, for example, the Ministry of Health, Labour and Welfare has developed career maps for a range of fields and industries, showing different possible career pathways. In the United States, the so-called *career pathways model* has been applied in several sectors, including health care, manufacturing, information technology, construction and shipping/logistics/transportation (Box 2.3). Interactions with employers, through site visits or information interviews, can be valuable for mid-career jobseekers or those facing employment transitions. The Career Transition Assistance programme in Australia, which targets mid-career jobseekers age 45+, emphasises employer visits for unemployed workers looking to transition into new sectors or occupations as a way to clarify which skills the employer is looking for (Box 2.6).

Mid-career adults may also benefit from certain types of labour market information. Given their greater family and financial responsibilities, mid-career adults may be less geographically mobile than younger adults. For them, information about local labour market and training opportunities will be crucial, as they will have less scope to travel or relocate for work or training. Career advisors need to have strong linkages with local employers and industry groups to understand their skill needs. Furthermore, having been in the labour market and away from initial education for many years, mid-career adults are distanced from the formal education and training system and could benefit from impartial information about training opportunities. Nearly a quarter (23%) of mid-career adult users of career guidance in Australia received guidance from an education or training provider, which is a higher share than observed across other countries in the survey (14%) (Figure 2.6). Guidance provided directly by an education and training institution is likely to be well-informed about training opportunities at that given institution. The risk is that the adult is not made aware of training opportunities at other institutions which might be a better fit for their particular training and career trajectory. Finally, with their complex family and work responsibilities, mid-career adults would benefit from information about flexible options for upskilling and reskilling, including training offered online, part-time or in micro-credential formats.

Effective career guidance for mid-career adults also needs to be responsive to their adult level concerns, including family and work responsibilities. Offering services during flexible hours or at community centres where childcare is available is helpful. Career guidance services for mid-career adults should also be well-linked to support services related to physical and mental health, financial advice, family and childcare support, and education and training guidance.

Box 2.2. Support for recognition of prior learning processes within career guidance in Finland

Adults who want to complete a competence-based qualification (CBQ) or a preparatory training for a competence-based qualification, can have their skills validated and receive support from a career guidance advisor in navigating the process. In order to complete a CBQ, candidates must demonstrate certain skills and competences required in the profession, outlined in the Requirements of Competence-based Qualifications defined by the Finnish National Board of Education. Education providers are responsible for providing personalised guidance and support to students as they carry out the validation process, and help them plan the next steps of their career. Adults receive a personalised learning plan that charts and recognises the skills they already have, those they need, and in which learning environments they can be acquired. Certificates are awarded by Qualification Committees (*Näyttötutkintotoimikunta),* which are sector-specific tripartite bodies that oversee the quality of the provision of CBQs.

Finally, how career guidance is delivered – whether face-to-face, by telephone or online, individually or in a group – deserves consideration when thinking about how mid-career adults could best be served. Face-to-face is the most common delivery method for career guidance in Australia (55% of mid-career adult users) (Figure 2.3). It might be thought that meeting with someone in person would be preferable for mid-career adults who may be less comfortable with digital channels (videoconference and online chat/portals). However, a significant share of mid-career adults declare that they would actually prefer to access career guidance via videoconference and online portals (Figure 2.3). From interviews, the OECD team heard that demand for career guidance programmes directed at mid-career adults (Skills Checkpoint for Older Workers) actually increased during the pandemic, despite having to switch from face-to-face to remote alternatives. Perhaps this reflects the greater flexibility these alternative channels afford to mid-career adults who have time constraints due to family and work responsibilities. The Career Transition Assistance programme in Australia places strong emphasis on group delivery. Group delivery is seen to be an important element in combatting potential shame that mid-career jobseekers may feel in looking for sustainable employment at an older age, by reminding them that they are not alone.

Figure 2.3. Actual and preferred channels of service delivery

Percentage of adults who spoke to a career guidance advisor over the past five years, by age, actual channel of delivery (Actual), and preferred channel of delivery (Preferred)

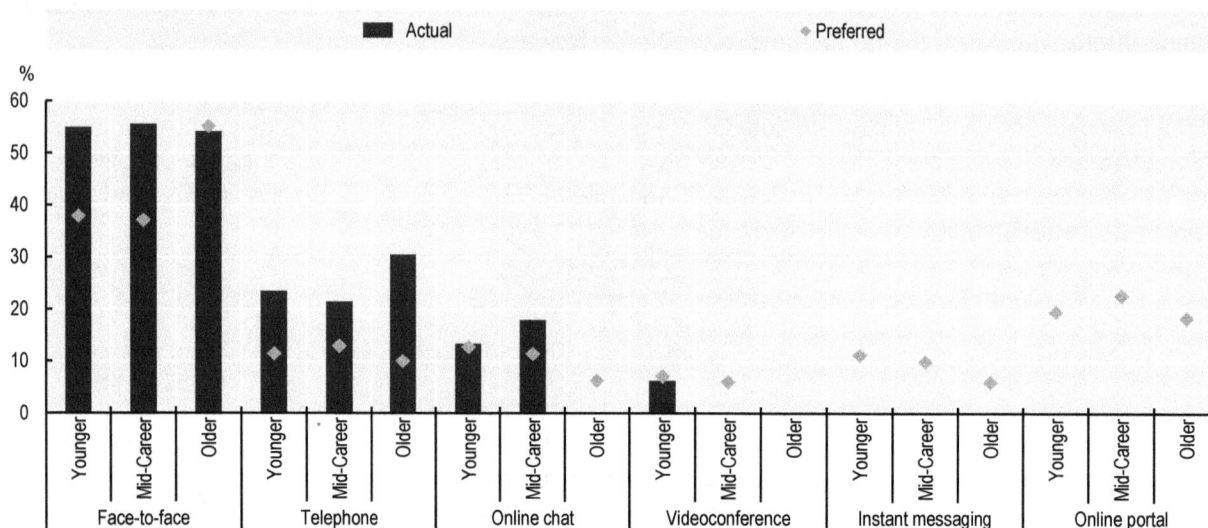

Note: Data refer to the last time the respondent spoke to a career guidance advisor. "Actual" refers to the percentage of people who spoke to a career guidance advisor over the past five years, by their actual channel of delivery. Online portal was not included in the list of possible delivery channels. "Preferred" refers to the percentage of all respondents, including both users and non-users of career guidance services, by their preferred channel of delivery. The younger group includes adults between the ages of 25 and 39, the mid-career group includes adults between the ages of 40 and 54, and the older group includes adults between the ages of 55 and 64. The value for some sub-groups was suppressed due to insufficient sample size (this applied to actual use of online chat for older adults, actual use of videoconference for mid-career and older, actual use of instant messaging for younger adults, mid-career adults and older adults, and preferred use of videoconference for older adults). Source: OECD 2020/2021 Survey of Career Guidance for Adults (SCGA).

Box 2.3. Testing the United States' "Career Pathways" model in Ontario, Canada

The Career Pathways model developed in the United States offers post-secondary education and training delivery through a series of modular steps, with each step leading to higher credentials and employment opportunities. This model aligns education, workforce development and support services to support learners to attain high quality and sustainable employment. The components of a Career Pathway include accelerated and accessible credentials and placement, support services, employer engagement and subsidised training programmes. A unique feature of this model is that the pathway has multiple entry and exit points, allowing individuals to enter at the most appropriate skill level and/or transition easily between participating in the labour market and pursuing further training. A review commissioned by the Department of Labor found that the health care sector most frequently implemented the Career Pathways model. Health care may be well suited to the Career Pathways model because there are clear occupational progressions, from entry-level (e.g. nursing aides, personal care aides), to mid-level (e.g. licensed and vocational nurses) to higher-level occupations (e.g. registered nurses, diagnostic-related technicians).

In Ontario, many lower-skilled adults find it difficult to access high quality jobs and employers struggle to find workers with the right skills. Recognising that the Career Pathways model has not been widely adopted outside the United States, the Ontario Centre for Workforce Innovation (OCWI) funded four projects focused on building the evidence base in Ontario. While none of the projects tested a fully developed Career Pathway, each project explored the development of some key features of the model.

The conclusion was that Career Pathways have the potential to meet skill needs in target sectors provided there is a deep understanding of the sector's skills needs. Strategic partnerships between employers, workforce development services, and education institutions are crucial for successful implementation. The assessment report concluded that future projects should focus on deepening partnerships with employers and labour market experts to identify sectors where the Career Pathways model could be effective.

Source: OCWI (2019[2]), "Career Pathways Demonstration Project: Final Report"; https://ocwi-coie.ca/wp-content/uploads/2019/03/Career-Pathways-Demonstration-Project-Final-Report-March-11.pdf, Palamar, M. and K. Pasolli (2018[3]), "Career Pathways" a promising model for skills training, Institute for Research on Public Policy; https://policyoptions.irpp.org/magazines/november-2018/career-pathways-promising-model-skills-training/, Sarna, M. and J. Strawn (2018[4]), "Career Pathways Implementation Synthesis: Career Pathways Design Study", https://www.dol.gov/sites/dolgov/files/OASP/legacy/files/3-Career-Pathways-Implementation-Synthesis.pdf.

2.2. What motivates mid-career adults to participate in career support?

Mid-career adults seek career guidance for different reasons, depending on where they are in their career or personal life, their employment status, and job ambitions. They may be looking for a new job, returning to the labour market after an absence, choosing a training or education programme, or consulting career guidance as part of receiving unemployment benefits or subsidised training. Chapter 1 reported that a relatively high share of mid-career adults in Australia use career guidance. However, some mid-career groups use career guidance much less than their counterparts, including low-educated adults, women, and foreign-born adults. This section looks at the reasons that adults pursue career guidance, the barriers that prevent some from consulting these services and why they choose one provider over another, with an aim to better understand how to motivate mid-career adults to use career support.

Compared to other countries in the SCGA, mid-career adults in Australia are more likely to seek career guidance to progress in their current job (43% vs. 30% in other countries) or to choose a study or training programme (37% vs. 25%) (Figure 2.4). This is consistent with the finding that Australian mid-career adults are more likely than those in other countries to receive guidance from their employer or from an education and training institution (Figure 2.6). Other reported reasons include looking for a job (33%), wanting to change jobs (32%), being required to (28%) or because one is uncertain about one's future labour market prospects (14%).

Figure 2.4. Mid-career adults' reasons for speaking with a career guidance advisor

Share of mid-career adults who spoke with a career guidance advisor over the past five years, by reason

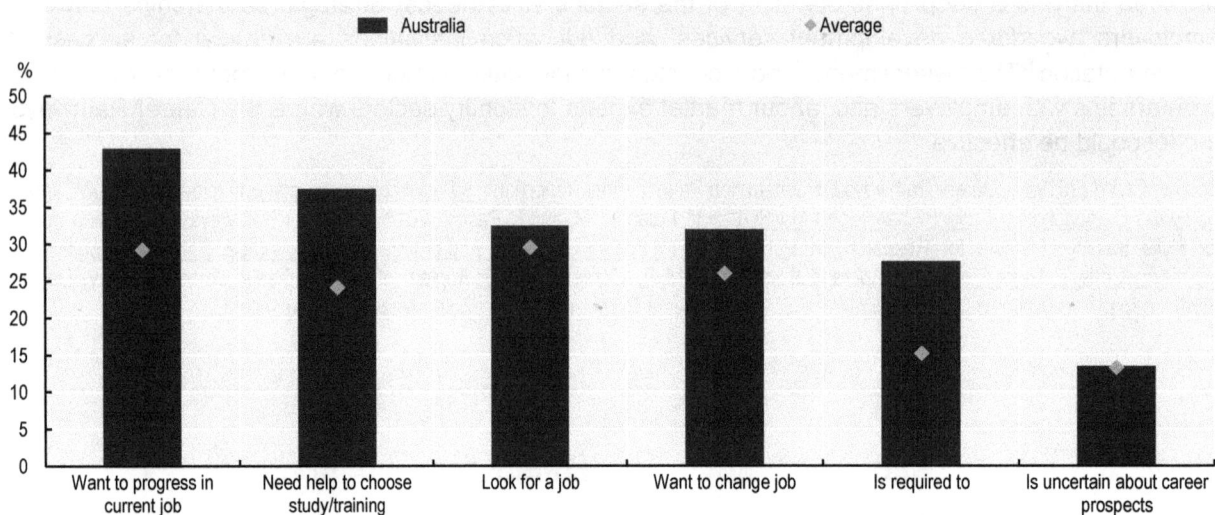

Note: Average includes Argentina, Australia, Brazil, Canada, Chile, France, Germany, Italy, Mexico, New Zealand and the United States. Respondents could choose more than one answer. Data refers to the last time the respondent spoke to a career guidance advisor. The mid-career group includes adults between the ages of 40 and 54.
Source: OECD 2020/2021 Survey of Career Guidance for Adults (SCGA).

Motivating mid-career adults to use career guidance starts with an understanding of why they do not use these services more. Figure 2.5 shows that among mid-career adults who did not speak with a career guidance advisor over the past five years, 50% of men and 60% of women did not feel the need to. These adults may already be established in their careers, not planning a change in their working lives or not interested in education and training opportunities. Another explanation is that they are not fully aware of or informed about the benefits of receiving professional career guidance. The higher incidence of women not feeling the need to see a career guidance advisor could be linked to traditional gender roles where women are encouraged to focus on family related responsibilities rather than career progression. About 21% of men and 19% of women non-users did not speak to a career guidance advisor because they did not know such services existed. This suggests either a lack of information about career guidance services (and a need for more efforts to promote these services), or that these services are not easily accessible.

Time constraints are a barrier for both men and women, but for different reasons. Ten percent of women reported not accessing career guidance due to time constraints related to family or childcare responsibilities, compared to only 4% of men. Offering career guidance in community centres or other places with childcare options is one way to tackle this barrier. Thirteen percent of mid-career men reported being too busy at work to access career guidance, compared to 4% of women. Supporting employer-provided career guidance can help tackle this barrier, especially for those who wish to progress within the same job. Another possible policy response to address time constraints could include career guidance in training vouchers that entitle adults to time off from work to pursue these activities. Both Denmark and the Netherlands allow individuals to use paid leave for education and training purposes towards career guidance visits.

Other barriers were more minor and similar for men and women: cost (4%), inconvenient time or place (2%), or poor quality (1%).

Figure 2.5. Reasons for not speaking with a career guidance advisor

Share of mid-career adults who did not speak with a career guidance advisor over the past five years, by gender and reason

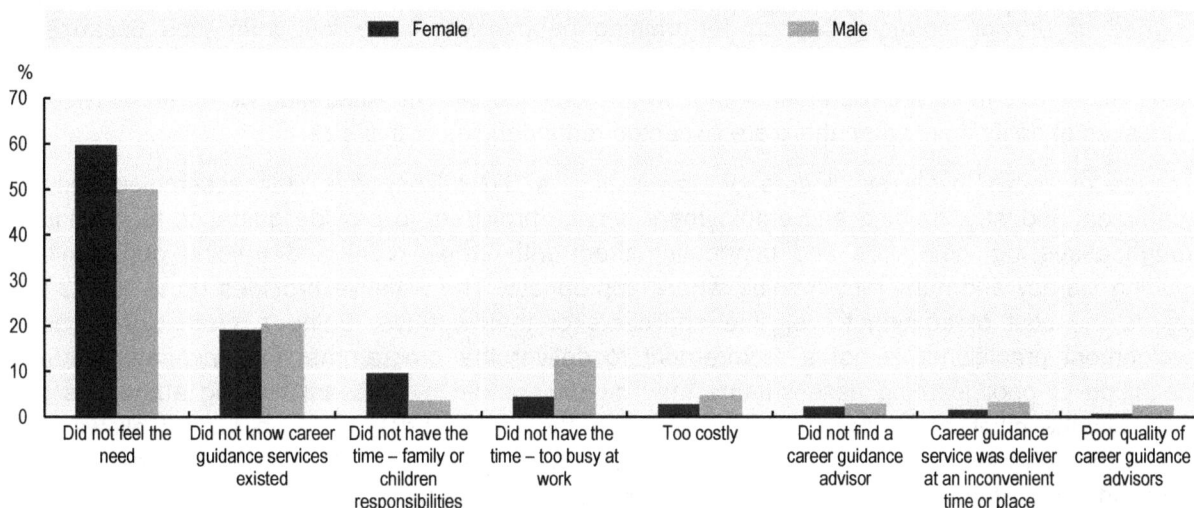

Notes: The mid-career group includes adults between the ages of 40 and 54.
Source: OECD 2020/2021 Survey of Career Guidance for Adults (SCGA).

Efforts are needed to reach out to adults who may not be aware that they could benefit from career guidance, or that such services exist. During interviews, stakeholders reported that the publicly funded employment service(PES) in most Australian states could do a better job of referring vulnerable adults to career guidance services. In addition to strong referral systems, the programmes which have experienced most success in connecting vulnerable adults with career guidance tend to have a strong link to the PES and enjoy strong state support, such as the Rapid Response Skills Initiative in Tasmania (Box 2.4) and Jobs Victoria Advocates (Box 2.7). Conducting outreach in hard-to-reach rural and remote communities is an important way to engage vulnerable adults in these communities, where services tend to be recommended via word of mouth.

Box 2.4. Career guidance services with outreach to vulnerable groups in Tasmania

The **Rapid Response Skills Initiative** in Tasmania is a career guidance programme that involves actively reaching out to individuals who are about to lose their jobs in situations of mass layoffs. Originally designed to provide financial support for training people who have lost their jobs because of retrenchment due to company closure, the programme was extended to include co-operation with businesses where there are redundancies of 15 or more people. The Australian Government requires businesses to notify them when there are expected redundancies of this size.

In cases of known business closure or downsizing, a Skills Response Unit assembles relevant government, industry, training and employment service providers to provide guidance to individuals through assessing their skills and connecting them with employment and training opportunities, including literacy and numeracy training where appropriate. The initiative provides up to AUD 3 000 towards the cost of training for eligible applicants or their spouse. Being a professional career development practitioner is not a requirement to deliver the programme. For mid-career adults, recognition of prior learning assessments may be undertaken by relevant training authorities and covered by the initiative. Providing career guidance early, before at-risk adults are laid off, allows them to think through their careers and make training and employment choices without the financial and mental pressure of unemployment. They also reap the benefits of more continuous income, as well as putting less pressure on jobactive and the unemployment insurance system.

2.3. Who is best placed to deliver career guidance services to mid-career adults?

In addition to how services are delivered, who delivers services is another important consideration in designing effective career guidance for mid-career adults. This section briefly discusses the role of the Career Industry Council of Australia (CICA) in establishing standards for the skills and qualifications of professional career development practitioners. It then reviews the types of providers currently delivering career guidance to adults in Australia, their strengths and weaknesses, and which group of mid-career adults could most benefit from their services.

Given their specialised knowledge and skills, professional career development practitioners may be best placed to deliver career guidance to mid-career adults. CICA has developed professional standards for career development practitioners (Box 2.5). Most public career guidance programmes in Australia do not have to be delivered by professional career development practitioners. The exceptions are Jobs Victoria Career Counsellors Service, Careers NSW, and the NCI (National Careers Institute) School Leavers Information Service. Given the complex needs of mid-career adults detailed above, there is a strong case for establishing quality standards for the qualifications and skills of career guidance professionals who deliver public services. While the professional standards developed by CICA are recognised as the benchmark for career development in Australia, the career guidance industry is not regulated on a federal level and there is limited use of CICA-registered career development practitioners in the publicly funded employment services or other public career guidance programmes. According to stakeholder interviews, private career guidance providers often employ professional career development practitioners, and employer-provided career guidance also often enlists the services of professional career development practitioners.

The rest of this section reviews the types of providers currently delivering career guidance to adults in Australia.

Box 2.5. Career Industry Council of Australia

The Career Industry Council of Australia (CICA) is a national peak body for the career industry in Australia. Its vision is to enhance transitions and productivity by advocating the individual, social and economic benefits of quality career development for all Australians. The organisation is a focal point for government and other stakeholders concerned for and interested in promoting quality career development services in Australia. CICA supports its member associations, develops guidance practice for professional career development practitioners, informs national and state-level policies and engages with key stakeholders.

CICA manages the Australian Register of Professional Career Development Practitioners. The Register, which has been operational since April 2022, is the single national point of reference for ensuring and promoting professional career development practitioners across the whole industry in Australia.

CICA has developed the Professional Standards for Australian Career Development Practitioners, which provides the foundation for industry standards. To enter the industry as a professional career development practitioner, advisors need a post-graduation qualification offered through a university or registered training organisation. CICA provides the opportunity for training providers to have their programmes endorsed. CICA endorsement ensures that programmes submitted by providers meet the need of the career development industry both from a quality assurance and skill development perspective. The content being delivered in the programme is mapped to the core competencies of the CICA Profession Standards.

CICA-registered career development professionals need to stay current about labour market developments to provide quality career guidance and maintain their membership with the organisation. The organisation provides ongoing professional learning linked to the core competencies of the Professional Standards.

The largest provider of career services for mid-career adults in Australia is the publicly funded employment service (PES), though for the most part these tend to offer job matching rather than career guidance. Nearly a quarter (24%) of mid-career adults who spoke with a career guidance advisor in the past five years did so through a publicly funded employment service (Figure 2.6). This is very close to the survey average (22%). PES services are well-suited to unemployed mid-career adults who need job matching support, where the aim is to get them quickly back into work. A focus on getting people back into work quickly has a number of advantages: it shortens the period they are without income, reduces their need for state-provided financial support, avoids scarring effects from unemployment, and may counter negative impacts on motivation and confidence from being idle. However, it runs the risk of matching people with unsustainable employment that is either of poor quality or a bad match with their skills and interests.

Figure 2.6. Providers of career guidance services for mid-career adults

Percentage of mid-career adults who spoke to a career guidance advisor over the past five years, by provider

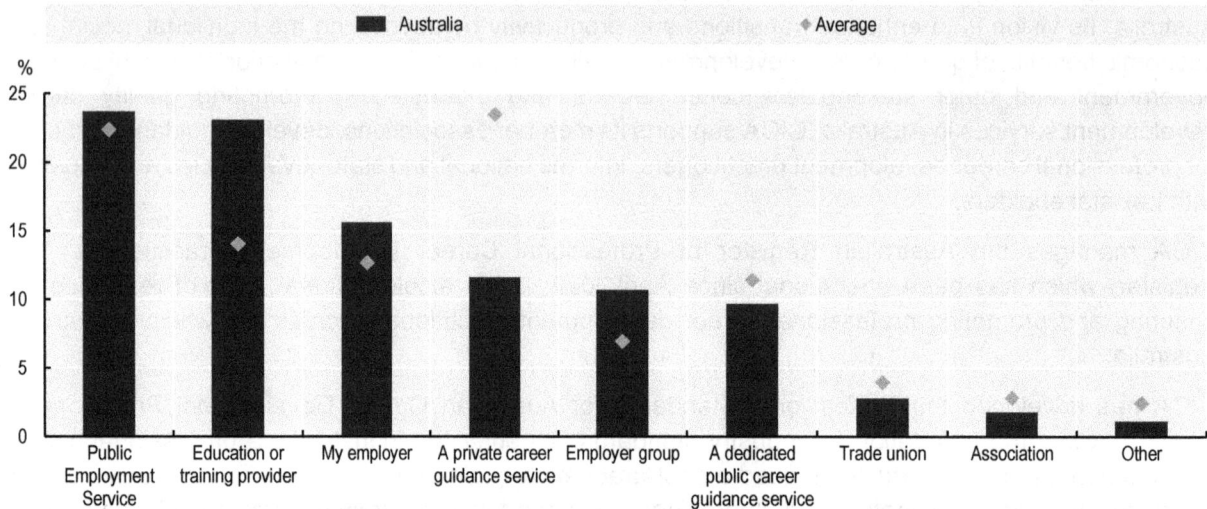

Note: Average includes Argentina, Australia, Brazil, Canada, Chile, France, Germany, Italy, Mexico, New Zealand and the United States. Data refers to the last time the respondent spoke to a career guidance advisor. The mid-career group includes adults between the ages of 40 and 54. Source: OECD 2020/2021 Survey of Career Guidance for Adults (SCGA).

Government-funded career guidance for unemployed adults who are referred by the PES is rare in Australia, with two notable exceptions: the federal Career Transition Assistance programme, and the Jobs Victoria Career Counsellors programme. To avoid duplication of services, unemployed adults participating in jobactive or another public service are not eligible for the Skills Checkpoint for Older Workers programme mentioned above. Australia's Career Transition Assistance (CTA) programme offers career guidance to jobseekers age 45+ who have been referred by jobactive. Participants in the 8-week programme have an initial meeting with a career guidance advisor who conducts an assessment of experience and skills, and at the end creates a career pathway plan to address the gaps. The client can choose to execute the plan themselves, or bring it to a PES counsellor for further assistance and follow-up. The programme relies on co-operation with local employers who share information on skills needs, and organise job visits. The CTA programme is delivered by third-party employment providers, and there is no requirement that it be delivered by professional career development practitioners. It also faces capacity constraints and not all mid-career jobseekers who need career guidance can receive it. In Victoria, the state-funded employment service recently launched a programme that refers jobseekers to certified career guidance service when needed (Box 2.7). Victoria stands out as a best practice in Australia, both in offering state-funded career guidance to all adults provided by professional career development practitioners, and in its efforts to actively reach out to adults who need support through the Jobs Victoria Mentors and Advocates programmes.

Box 2.6. Federal-level Career Transition Assistance programme

Australia's Career Transition Assistance (CTA) programme offers career guidance to jobseekers age 45 and over. Participants in the 8-week programme have an initial meeting with a facilitator (a career guidance advisor) who conducts a Career Pathway Assessment of experience and skills, and at the end creates a Career Pathway Plan (CPP) to address gaps. Following completion of CTA, providers conduct a handover meeting with the participant and their referring provider to discuss next steps as outlined in the CPP.

The group setting is central to CTA service delivery, and provides participants with the opportunity for networking and peer support. The programme also relies on co-operation with local employers who share information on skills needs and organise job visits. Part of the course involves identifying transferable skills, understanding the labour market needs of the local area, and tailoring applications to local job opportunities.

CTA is closely connected to jobactive and some providers offer jobactive services as well. There is no requirement that CTA services be delivered by professional career development practitioners. Providers have some independence in designing the assessment format for the programme they deliver, though improving digital literacy is a common focus.

During the pandemic, providers had to pivot to a hybrid delivery, which combined in-person and digital delivery. Digital literacy is a core component of the course, and transitioning to digital delivery was a challenge for many clients who did not possess these skills, and needed a basic level of digital literacy to access the service. Providers who utilised a range of delivery methods were most successful at reaching mature clients with low digital skills. The programme resumed face-to-face delivery where local COVID-19 restrictions were lifted.

Box 2.7. Career guidance programmes offered in Victoria

Started in August 2021, the **Jobs Victoria Career Counsellors Service** (JVCCS) is delivered by the Career Education Association of Victoria (CEAV) on behalf of the Victorian Government. Personalised guidance sessions are offered free of charge on an appointment basis, and all career counsellors must be professionally endorsed by the Career Industry Council of Australia (CICA). The offer is open to all adults regardless of their employment status, and jobseekers can be referred to the service by Jobs Victoria (state-funded employment service). The programme employs 36 professional career development practitioners, as well as counsellors specialised in working with Aboriginal communities and those with disabilities. Services may be delivered face-to-face, via phone or video platform, depending on the needs and preferences of the clients. CEAV-trained counsellors hold post-secondary graduate qualifications in career development, and must maintain professional membership with a career industry association and participate in ongoing professional development.

CEAV-trained career guidance counsellors are also located in **Skills and Jobs Centres**. Skills and Jobs Centres are one-stop-shops that are based in technical and further education institutions (TAFEs) and provide free expert advice on training and employment opportunities, including career guidance, training, referrals to welfare support and financial advice, assistance in recognition of prior learning and information on employment trends and skills shortages. The Centres also engage with a broad range of local industries.

> **Jobs Victoria Advocates** perform active outreach at the local level to anyone who needs assistance to identify and access services related to employment, and currently employs 108 advocates across Victoria. The outreach model is particularly valuable in engaging hard-to-reach and vulnerable groups in Victoria including long-term job seekers, unemployed people with labour market barriers, refugees, and asylum seekers. Advocates connect with people in everyday locations: libraries, community centres, public housing foyers, shopping centres and other community services. Many Advocates are multilingual, further enabling them to connect with diverse community members. They provide referrals to employment, training and related services in Victoria, including career guidance.
>
> The **Jobs Victoria Mentor** service targets jobseekers facing barriers to employment. There are more than 50 services funded across the state, targeting locations with high labour market needs. Core services include job-seeking and training assistance, assistance with personal needs and connection to other community service. The programme targets ex-offenders, refugees and asylum seekers, migrants with professional qualifications, Aboriginal jobseekers and young people with complex barriers to employment.
>
> Jobs Victoria Advocates, Career Counsellors and the Mentor service are managed by Jobs Victoria, an initiative of the Victorian State Government Department of Jobs, Precincts and Regions. Skills and Jobs Centres are managed by the Department of Education and Training Victoria. Both departments collaborate to ensure inclusive coverage and services in Victoria.

Education or training institutions are well placed to offer career guidance to mid-career adults who are already aware they need training. Some 23% of mid-career adults receive career guidance through an education or training institution in Australia, which is above the overall survey average (15%). A possible risk with career guidance provided by such institutions is that the advice they provide is biased by which training courses are available at their particular institution. Given that most mid-career adults have been out of formal education for many years, they could benefit from impartial information and advice about available training courses across institutions and which would be the best fit given their career aspirations. Education or training institutions might also have difficulty reaching adults who are not motivated to train, or who need career guidance to better conceptualise what career transitions they want to make prior to selecting a training course.

Career guidance provided by employers and employer groups is well suited to mid-career adults who wish to progress in their current occupation and company. In Australia, 16% of mid-career adults accessed career guidance services through their employer and 11% through an employer group (13% and 7% of mid-career adults in the countries covered by the SCGA used these providers, respectively). Generally, employers can provide guidance to workers about their career development opportunities within the company, and employer groups tend to be well informed about sectoral skills needs. They can assist employees to reflect on their career goals and find suitable training options in order to develop their skills. In addition to having good knowledge of the skill demands in their company and sector, employers often have good processes for recognising the employees' skills, as they have observed their performance. In Japan, the government encourages employers to provide career counselling services to their workers. This allows the employer to retain workers who might wish to change occupation, while allowing workers to better align their role and tasks to their career ambition, and to avoid disruptions in income that might occur if they attempted to retrain for a different role at a different company (OECD, 2021[5]). Two limitations with employer-provided guidance are that it tends to favour high-performing employees, and does not support job transitions, as the employer has an incentive to retain the employee. Some exceptions do apply in Australia: in case of large-scale industry-specific closures, such as in the automotive sector, job transition centres have been set up inside the company to support transitions for workers. Career guidance has been a key element of this service (OECD, 2019[6]).

For mid-career adults seeking to change firm or sector, a private career guidance provider may be the option best suited to their needs. In comparison to other countries covered by the SCGA, Australian adults use private career guidance providers much less. Only 12% of mid-career adults in Australia used career guidance services offered by a private career guidance provider, compared to an average of 23% of mid-career adults in other countries covered by the survey. There is no centralised register for private professional career development practitioners, though CICA plans to develop one in April 2022. To date, practitioners have relied on self-promotion and outreach to attract clients. Private career guidance providers are more impartial than employers or education and training institutions, and they have an overview of labour market information for a variety of sectors. As private career guidance advisors have to compete for their clients, they have a strong incentive to complete the qualification and training requirements to attain and maintain professional certification through CICA, as this is a mark of quality. An important aspect to consider is that private career services are commonly paid for by the individual. Unless subsidised, career guidance from private providers may be costly and out of reach for mid-career adults with financial constraints or in precarious employment.

Some OECD countries have dedicated public career guidance services that are specialised in delivering career guidance and are at least partly government funded. Relative to the PES which has many roles other than providing career guidance, this is the sole mission of dedicated public career guidance services. They are also more independent than the PES, as their service is not motivated by the individual entering a job quickly. In France, the *Conseil en Evolution Professionelle* (CEP) is a dedicated public career guidance provider open to all individuals regardless of their employment status. The CEP is a career guidance hub: adults can browse the CEP webpage to find a qualified career guidance advisor who meets their needs and all career guidance offered through CEP is free of charge for all individuals. The 10% of mid-career adults who reported accessing career guidance services through a dedicated public career guidance service may have been referring to either the state-level Jobs Victoria Career Counselling Service, the Tasmania Rapid Response Skills Initiative, or the federal-level Skills Checkpoint for Older Workers, Career Transition Assistance or the Mid-Career Checkpoint programmes (Box 2.1).

Finally, some associations or community organisations offer career guidance to unemployed or low-skilled individuals, often free of charge as part of public programmes. In Australia, only 3% of mid-career adults received services this way.

2.3. How should career guidance for mid-career adults be funded?

Given the shared private and public benefits to career guidance for mid-career adults, a case can be made to share the cost between individuals, employers and government. Adults are the direct beneficiaries of career guidance services, making their individual contributions justified. However, there are also public benefits to career guidance – including better skills matching and more productive and resilient economies – that justify public investment. While employers may be reluctant to provide career guidance out of fear of losing productive employees to possible new roles outside of their company, they can benefit from better skills matching within their firm, as well as lower turnover.

Mid-career adults in Australia are more likely to report paying for career services out-of-pocket than are those in other surveyed countries. In Australia, 57% of mid-career users of career guidance paid out-of-pocket for the services they received, compared to the overall average of 33% (Figure 2.7). Australia is also one of only a few countries where mid-career adults are more likely to pay out-of-pocket than the total adult population. Since relatively few mid-career adults consult private career guidance services (only 12% of users), it is not clear why the out-of-pocket rate is so high. Perhaps respondents interpreted "paying for career guidance" as paying for related services. For instance, if they paid an education or training provider for a training programme, perhaps they understand this to mean paying indirectly for the career guidance they received through their education or training provider. Even though mid-career adults in Australia are more likely to pay out-of-pocket for the services they received, cost appears to be a negligible barrier to accessing career guidance services (only 4% of non-users reported cost to be a barrier, Figure 2.5).

Figure 2.7. Mid-career adults' out of pocket contribution to career guidance

Share of mid-career adults who paid (partially or fully) for career guidance services

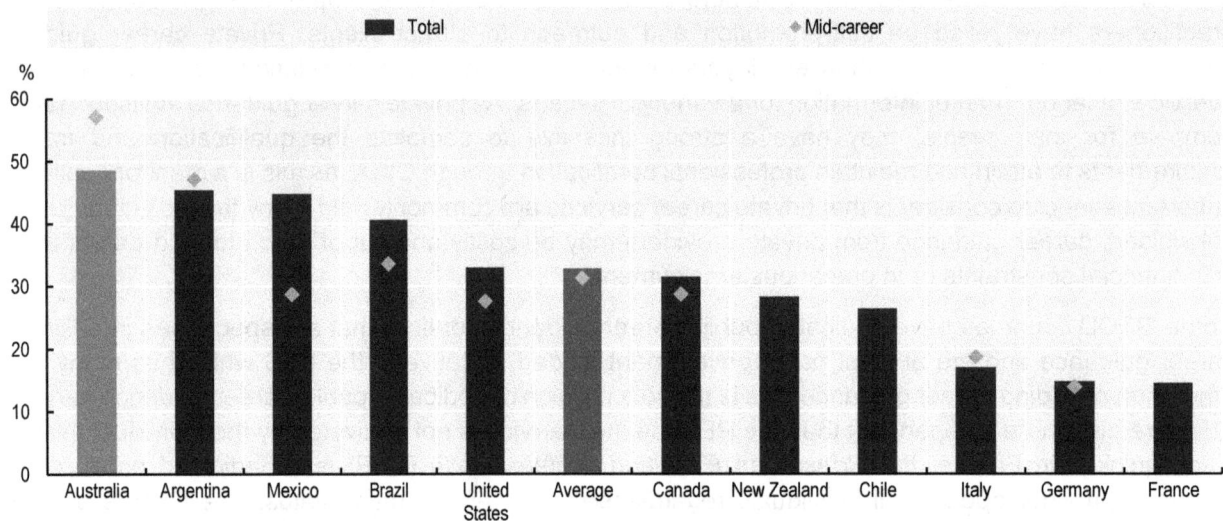

Note: Average includes Argentina, Australia, Brazil, Canada, Chile, France, Germany, Italy, Mexico, New Zealand and the United States. Data refers to the last time the respondent spoke to a career guidance advisor. The mid-career group includes adults between the ages of 40 and 54. Values suppressed for mid-career adults in New Zealand, Chile and France as there were less than 30 observations. Total population refers to all adults aged 25 to 64 in the survey.
Source: OECD 2020/2021 Survey of Career Guidance for Adults (SCGA).

Adults in more precarious employment situations are much less likely to pay out-of-pocket for career guidance than those who are employed full-time. Survey results show that 78% of full-time employed mid-career adults in Australia who received career guidance report paying (fully or partially) for it, while only (2%) of unemployed adults, retired adults, and other adults who are out of the labour force and who received career guidance report paying for it. That said, since unemployed adults largely report receiving career guidance through the publicly funded employment service (whether federally funded or state-funded), they tend to receive job matching rather than career guidance services.

Currently, there are no schemes to promote co-funding of private career guidance between individuals and the government in Australia. The full cost of private career guidance services is thus borne by the individual, which hinders access for those who cannot afford it. This concerns not only the direct cost of the guidance services, but also the opportunity cost associated with taking time away from work to speak with a career guidance advisor. Career vouchers, used in Belgium and Germany, are one way to support co-funding (Box 2.1). In Germany, only unemployed adults are eligible for the career voucher, while in Belgium any employed adult is eligible after having worked a minimum number of hours with a given employer. In the Netherlands, workers age 45+ were temporarily eligible for subsidised career guidance as part of a pilot initiative (Box 2.9).

Schemes to encourage employers to contribute to the cost of career guidance services for adults are rare. Japan is one example, where until 2018 employers who implemented the "self-career dock system" could receive government subsidies to offer individual and group counselling.

The Australian Government should consider introducing financial incentives to promote co-funding of private career guidance services. Such financial incentives could be directed at all adults, or restricted to those who have the strongest need for career guidance or for whom financial barriers are highest, such as those in more precarious employment situations.

Box 2.8. Career guidance vouchers in Flanders and Germany

Flanders

In the Flanders and Brussels region of Belgium, employed adults have access to career guidance vouchers (*loopbaancheques*) to consult accredited career counsellors. Every six years, adults can request vouchers for seven hours of counselling (one voucher of four hours and one of three hours). The second voucher can only be used if the first four hours of guidance have been completed, and can be used with the same or a different provider. Only adults who are employed (employees and self-employed) at the time of the request and have at least seven years of work experience can access the vouchers. The full voucher amount (expressed in hours) needs to be used within a period of 12 months. The vouchers are managed by the public employment service. In 2018, 24 741 adults used a career guidance voucher. To be eligible, one must have worked a minimum number of hours with a one's current employer.

Adults pay EUR 40 per voucher (i.e. EUR 40 for the first four hours and EUR 40 for the last three hours). As the vouchers have a value of EUR 169 per hour, the government subsidises a large share of the costs. Before adults decide which accredited guidance counsellor to use, they can get a free introduction session with the counsellor. This can help the individual make informed choices about which provider to choose. Once the adult has selected their counsellor, the counselling consists of i) an assessment of strengths, weaknesses, interest and aspirations, ii) analysis of career objectives, iii) development of a personalised career plan, and ii) advice and guidance on how to implement the career plan. The participants can get a free follow-up session (in addition to the sessions paid by their vouchers) with their counsellor up to 12 months after the end of their counselling sessions.

Germany

The German Federal Employment Agency (*Bundesagentur für Arbeit*) grants jobseekers an "activation and placement voucher" (*Aktivierungs- und Vermittlungsgutschein*) when they meet minimum eligibility requirements. The placement officer defines the objective of the voucher and attaches a funding commitment. The jobseeker can then choose between guidance counselling and training courses and use the voucher to pay the provider directly.

Source: OECD 2020 Policy Questionnaire, 'Career Guidance for Adults'; www.arbeitsagentur.de/aktivierungs-vermittlungsgutschein-avgs;

Box 2.9. Subsidised career guidance for mid-career adults in the Netherlands

In the Netherlands, workers aged 45+ who work at least 12 hours per week temporarily had access to free personalised career guidance (*Ontwikkeladvies*). The programme was developed as a temporary measure, starting from December 2017 until July 2020. During that period, 25 800 requests for subsidies were submitted.

The goal of the programme was to help mid-career workers assess their personal strengths, needs, and opportunities in order to develop a better understanding of what they want, can do and the opportunities available to ensure that they can stay in employment until retirement age.

To participate in the subsidised guidance programme, workers needed to find a suitable guidance counsellor. The selected counsellor was in charge of requesting the subsidy (EUR 600) from the government. The sessions were confidential, and the employer was not informed of the worker's participation in the programme. The counsellor developed a personalised development plan for the participant, based on their interests, skills, needs and aspirations. Guidance could be provided by private career counselling providers or by trade unions.

Source: OECD (2021[5]), *Creating Responsive Adult Learning Opportunities in Japan*, https://dx.doi.org/10.1787/cfe1ccd2-en.

References

Fialho, P., G. Quintini and M. Vandeweyer (2019), "Returns to different forms of job related training: Factoring in informal learning", *OECD Social, Employment and Migration Working Papers*, No. 231, OECD Publishing, Paris, https://doi.org/10.1787/b21807e9-en. [1]

OCWI (2019), *Career Pathways Demonstration Project: Final Report*, Ontario Centre for Workplace Innovation, https://ocwi-coie.ca/wp-content/uploads/2019/03/Career-Pathways-Demonstration-Project-Final-Report-March-11.pdf. [2]

OECD (2021), *Creating Responsive Adult Learning Opportunities in Japan*, Getting Skills Right, OECD Publishing, Paris, https://doi.org/10.1787/cfe1ccd2-en. [5]

OECD (2019), *Financial Incentives to Promote Adult Learning in Australia*, Getting Skills Right, OECD Publishing, Paris, https://doi.org/10.1787/c79badcc-en. [6]

Palamar, M. and K. Pasolli (2018), ""Career Pathways" a promising model for skills training, Institute for Research on Public Policy", https://policyoptions.irpp.org/magazines/november-2018/career-pathways-promising-model-skills-training/. [3]

Sarna, M. and J. Strawn (2018), *Career Pathways Implementation Synthesis: Career Pathways Design Study*, https://www.dol.gov/sites/dolgov/files/OASP/legacy/files/3-Career-Pathways-Implementation-Synthesis.pdf. [4]

<u>3</u> An assessment of career guidance for mid-career adults in Australia

This chapter reviews the Australian system of career guidance for mid-career adults and makes recommendations for how it could be strengthened. It provides a brief overview of how the overall system of career guidance for adults is co-ordinated, and then analyses provision for different sub-groups.

In Brief

Australia has several public career guidance programmes for mid-career adults, but the system faces challenges in co-ordination, awareness building and scale

Australia has public career guidance programmes that aim at mid-career adults, but improvements could be made to increase their uptake. The main findings from this chapter are:

- There are many actors involved in shaping and delivering career guidance services for mid-career adults in Australia. The National Career Institute (NCI) could raise awareness of available career guidance services, and the value of consulting career guidance regularly throughout one's career journey. Introducing financial support schemes could encourage co-funding of private career guidance between employed individuals, employers and the government.

- Australia has several programmes that target mid-career adults who face disruption or job transition, and these should be evaluated, and scaled up if evaluation results suggest they are successful. Proactive career guidance initiatives targeted at workers in declining industries have been successful in connecting workers with upskilling and reskilling opportunities and new employment. Yet, more outreach is necessary to connect other vulnerable groups with career guidance

- For unemployed mid-career adults, access to federally funded career guidance programmes is limited. Some of these individuals require more comprehensive career support than simply job matching. There is limited use of professional career development practitioners in public career guidance programmes (such as the Mid-Career Checkpoint, Skills Checkpoint for Older Workers and Career Transition Assistance programmes).

- Mid-career adults who are employed and not facing disruption can also benefit from career guidance – even if they do not feel the need for it, as survey results suggest. The NCI could raise awareness of the value of accessing career guidance throughout people's career journey, and not only when they are facing job disruption.

Introduction

This chapter reviews the Australian system of career guidance for mid-career adults. It provides a brief overview of how the overall system of career guidance for adults is co-ordinated, and then analyses provision for three sub-groups of mid-career adults: those who are employed and not facing job disruption, those who are employed and facing job disruption, and those who are unemployed or out of the labour force. The chapter makes recommendations about how each of these sub-groups of mid-career adults could be better served, as well as how the overall system could be strengthened.

3.1. Overall system of career guidance for mid-career adults in Australia

Australia has a federal structure, with responsibilities for career guidance for adults divided between the Commonwealth and the six states and two territories (hereafter referred to collectively as "states"). There are currently two federally funded career guidance programmes specifically targeting mid-career adults:

the Skills Checkpoint for Older Workers and the Mid-Career Checkpoint (Box 2.1). The federal government is also currently carrying out a pilot to provide job seekers, including those who are in mid-career, with one free career guidance session with a professional career development practitioner over the phone. In addition to these federally funded employment services, public career guidance for mid-career adults is provided through state-funded employment services, higher education institutions, technical and further education institutions (TAFEs) and other vocational education and training institutions. Western Australia used to have a central public career service that employed qualified career professionals, but this closed in 2018. Victoria is now the only state offering public career guidance through its state-funded employment services. New South Wales also started a pilot initiative in October 2021 (Careers NSW) to offer free career guidance to adults living in certain regions within the state.

With so many actors involved, co-ordination of career guidance policy is a challenge. The National Careers Institute (NCI) was established in 2019 to provide Australians of all ages and career stages with information and resources to navigate career pathways (Box 3.1). Part of its mandate is to strengthen and consolidate careers information, encourage collaboration and improve co-ordination between the various actors involved.

Box 3.1. Australia's National Career Institute

The National Careers Institute (NCI) is an entity that sits within the Department of Education, Skills and Employment and is tasked with being a source of independent careers information for Australians of all ages. Formed by the Australian Government following the 2019-20 federal budget measure, the NCI's Strategic Plan aims to support a strong and effective career information system.

Since its inception in 2019, the NCI has delivered a careers information portal (yourcareer.gov.au), administered a partnership grant programme, promoted VET, and administered a training and skills website (training.gov.au and My Skills website). The NCI was not intended to be a provider of career guidance, though it did set up and administer telephone-based career guidance through the School Leavers Information Service as a response to high youth unemployment during the COVID-19 pandemic.

The NCI works with industry and employers to better understand the changing nature of the workforce and promote information for employee development including upskilling and reskilling opportunities. The NCI also works across the Commonwealth Government and with state governments on career information and guidance-related matters.

The NCI could play a role in making adults more aware of available career guidance providers and the services they offer. This is a key challenge, because as highlighted in Chapter 2, 56% of mid-career non-users did not feel the need to speak to a career guidance advisor, while 20% of non-users did not speak to a career guidance advisor because they did not know such services existed. Public awareness campaigns can help to promote career guidance as a useful tool at any stage in one's career, to develop career management skills and build resiliency. In Flanders (Belgium), career guidance measures are supported by large media campaigns, such as the *En alles beweegt"* ("And everything is moving") campaign in 2020. Adults in Australia could also benefit from a central navigation tool that clearly states the career guidance programmes they are eligible for, given their state and employment status. Finally, building an evidence base about the importance of career guidance could also help to raise awareness of its value. The NCI initiated the National Careers Information Survey in 2022 as a one-off national survey to better understand the experiences and use of career information in Australia. Repeating this survey periodically, with the addition of questions related to the use of career guidance services, could potentially identify trends in take-up and experiences of career guidance services over time.

There are currently no schemes to promote co-funding of private career guidance between individuals, employers and the government in Australia. The share of adults in Australia who pay out of pocket (57%) is much higher than the average of other countries in the survey (31%). Adults in precarious employment situations such as casual, contract or part-time employment are much less likely to pay out-of-pocket for career guidance than those who are employed full time. There are strong arguments to justify employer and government investment in career guidance, including the associated benefits to these parties in terms of lower skills mismatch, higher productivity and employee retention. Career guidance vouchers, which are offered in both Flanders (Belgium) and Germany (Box 2.4), are one way to promote co-funding of career guidance between the individual and government. In France, funding available under individual training accounts can be used to pay for career guidance services. Both Denmark and the Netherlands allow individuals to use paid leave for education and training purposes towards career guidance visits, which is a type of co-funding between the individual and the employer.

There is potential for better and clearer pathways into career guidance for mid-career adults. In Australia, career guidance is often a standalone service that adults have to seek out. Better referral systems between services could both raise awareness about career guidance among mid-career adults, and also improve the quality of services. During interviews, Australian stakeholders called for stronger referral systems within the career and training system, with bridges between career guidance services, health services, financial advice, and family and childcare support. Career guidance counsellors are increasingly asked to support adults with complex barriers to employment, and a stronger referral system could enable better service.

The following sections will consider how Australia's current system of career guidance for adults could be strengthened for three distinct groups: employed mid-career adults who are not facing disruption, employed mid-career adults who are facing disruption, and mid-career adults who are unemployed or out of the labour force.

> **Box 3.2. Recommendations to strengthen co-ordination of career guidance for mid-career adults**
>
> - **Raising awareness about available career guidance services, and the benefits of such services for adults at any stage of their career. The NCI could take the lead in these activities.** As a hub for career-related information, the NCI could create a central navigation tool that clearly spells out which career guidance programmes are available to adults across the country based on their state and current employment status. The NCI could also promote career guidance not only as something for young people or jobseekers, but also as a service that could be beneficial for people of all ages and career stages, creating a stronger culture around lifelong learning and the role of career guidance throughout a person's career. Further, the NCI could contribute evaluation evidence on the impact of career guidance for mid-career adults, and in particular, identify which services are most effective for this target group. Repeating the National Careers Information Survey periodically would support these efforts.
>
> - **Introduce financial support schemes to promote co-funding, and reduce the individual cost of private career guidance.** Australia has the highest incidence of out-of-pocket payment among countries in the survey, and cost can be a barrier for adults in precarious employment. Financial support schemes, like career vouchers or public career guidance services, would reduce barriers for adults in precarious employment.
>
> - **Strengthen referral systems into and from career guidance services.** With their complex needs, mid-career adults can benefit from referrals to support services related to funding, health, financial planning, child and elder care, recognition of prior learning, and training. Stronger referral systems would also help to raise awareness about career guidance services among mid-career adults.

3.2. Career guidance for mid-career adults facing job disruption and job transitions

Mid-career adults facing job disruption and potential loss of employment – either due to automation, the green transition, or other trends affecting the labour market – could benefit from the support of career guidance in facilitating their employment transitions. Chapter 1 showed how mid-career adults in occupations with a higher risk of automation change occupation more often than those in lower risk occupations. However, they train less than mid-career adults in lower risk occupations. Career guidance can connect at-risk individuals to appropriate upskilling and reskilling opportunities, and help them to navigate a rapidly changing labour market and to find sustainable employment.

Both Tasmania's Rapid Response Skills Initiative and the federal Skills Checkpoint for Older Workers target employed adults who are at risk of losing their job. As of October 2021, Careers NSW is also offering a pilot programme allowing adults in certain regions of NSW to book a free appointment with a professional career development practitioner. They can also book an appointment with an industry expert in the industry they are considering transitioning into. These programmes involve proactively supporting adults before they lose their jobs, which allows them to make training and employment choices without the financial and mental pressure of unemployment. Both programmes involve speaking to a career guidance advisor who aids the clients in assessing their skills and evaluating the gap between their current skills and those in-demand in the local labour market. Tasmania's Rapid Response Skills Initiative includes support for recognition of prior learning, which can be a useful tool in formalising skills acquired through work experience in order to shorten training pathways into new sectors or occupations. Following the completion of the programmes and assessment of skills gaps, both programmes give mid-career adults suggestions for further training and offer funding to cover this training. While the combination of early intervention, use of skill assessments and recognition of prior learning, and support for training are promising programme features, evaluations have not been performed for either programme. Carrying out evaluations could inform efforts to improve these programmes and to scale up similar initiatives across the country. Building evidence about what works is the aim of the Future Skills Centre in Canada, which put out a call for proposals to test initiatives that support the upskilling and reskilling of mid-career adults (Box 3.3). A limitation of both the Rapid Response Skills Initiative and the federal Skills Checkpoint for Older Workers programmes is that because they do not have to be delivered by professional career development practitioners, they are not. Their impact is also limited, as the Rapid Response Initiative is only available in the state of Tasmania and the Skills Checkpoint for Older Workers is currently capped at 10 000 adults per year, though the cap has never been reached.

Mid-career adults who are facing disruption may benefit from active outreach in order to connect them with career support. This is important given that over half of mid-career adults do not feel they need career guidance, and another 20% are not aware that services exist. Jobs Victoria Advocates are trained by the Career Education Association of Victoria (CEAV) to reach out to adults in their own communities in order to connect them with social and employment services, including career guidance (Box 2.7). In Tasmania, the Rapid Response Skills Initiative mentioned above involves reaching out to workers in companies undergoing mass layoffs to offer career guidance and retraining opportunities. Australia has also previously implemented sector-wide initiatives during the closure of the auto-manufacturing industry: the Skills and Training initiative helped workers prepare to transition to new jobs in high demand sectors and occupations in affected regions. In the case of the Holden and Toyota plant closures, Transition Centres were set up within the plants. The Transition Centres offered career guidance, retraining opportunities, skills assessments and recognition of prior learning (OECD, 2018[1]). The initiatives were highly successful in helping employees find new employment.

Box 3.3. EDGE UP pilot for mid-career adults in Canada

The Energy to Digital Growth Education and Upskilling Project (EDGE UP) was developed by Calgary Economic Development in partnership with the Information and Communication Technology Council (ICTC) with the goal of reskilling displaced mid-career oil and gas professionals and helping them reemploy in emerging technology opportunities across all industries in Calgary. The EDGE UP team received financial support from the Future Skills Centre for the design, implementation and evaluation of the pilot.

The programme, modelled around ICTC's iAdvance workforce development approach, includes skills mapping and short duration workplace readiness training, technical training (such as IT Project Management, Data Analytics and Software Development), micro credentialing, and employment support. The EDGE UP team created reskilling pathways based on a skills mapping research study that highlighted the transferrable skills of the target population and their skills gaps when compared with the needs of the most in-demand digital occupations. After participants finished the training programme, they continued to receive ongoing employment support and job search assistance, including notifications about employment opportunities and check-in calls from the programme co-ordinator.

The programme evaluation was based on analyses of participant administrative data and participant surveys (baseline, exit and follow-up), as well as qualitative interviews with participants, programme partners and employers. There were 98 participants in the pilot, and 20 of them were interviewed as part of the evaluation.

Participants reported having clearer career goals following the participation in the programme. Half of the survey respondents reported being employed nine months after the completion of the programme, while 17% were enrolled in education or training programmes. The programme evaluation suggested that providing work placement opportunities and wraparound employment support would likely increase participants' chances of being hired and hiring professional career advisors could build stronger capacity in employment support.

Source: Blueprint (2022[2]), "Energy to Digital Growth Education and Upskilling Project (EDGE UP)" Evaluation Report, February 2022, Future Skills Centre, https://global-uploads.webflow.com/5f80fa46a156d5e9dc0750bc/62013a2147ce61c6ef0397ec_FSC-EDGEUP-Final.pdf.

Box 3.4. Recommendations to support mid-career adults facing disruption or job transitions

- **Scale up current programmes that target mid-career adults who are employed and at risk of losing their job.** Australia's current career guidance programmes for mid-career adults, Skills Checkpoint for Older Workers and the Mid-Career Checkpoint pilot, provide valuable support to this target group. The following actions should be taken to ensure the quality and success of these programmes as they are scaled up: i) first evaluate the impact of the programmes thus far; ii) make modifications as needed to the programmes to tailor them even further to the needs of mid-career adults; and iii) expand the programmes while building awareness of the benefits of career guidance for mid-career adults.

- **Support flexible and shorter career and learning pathways of mid-career adults who are facing disruption by better linking career guidance with recognition of prior learning**, as is currently done in Tasmania with the Rapid Response Skills Initiative. Allow funding for training that is tied to career guidance programmes to be used for recognition of prior learning processes. This would give adults formal recognition for skills acquired outside of formal training, and could shorten the time needed to retrain, thus facilitating their transitions.

- **Scale up efforts to reach out to potentially vulnerable adults, such as low-educated adults, those in part-time employment, foreign-born adults, or those living in rural areas, to connect them with career guidance.** Adults are often unaware of career guidance opportunities and their benefits. Victoria's approach of reaching out to and building relationships with potentially vulnerable adults in the community (e.g. in libraries, community centres) is a promising way to connect vulnerable adults with career guidance services, and could be scaled up across the country. Training and employing career guidance advisors who are from similar socio-economic backgrounds as vulnerable adults is another way to improve inclusivity of career services. This may be particularly effective in engaging Indigenous adults and those with disabilities, as Victoria is currently doing.

3.3. Career guidance for mid-career adults who are unemployed or out of the labour force

Career guidance can help unemployed mid-career adults find sustainable work. It encourages them to reflect on their skills and career aspirations, to identify relevant job opportunities and to find training opportunities in case of skills gaps. Adults with more complex barriers to employment can receive tailored support to overcome these barriers, thus avoiding long-term unemployment or a succession of poorly fitting jobs and subsequent unemployment spells.

For the most part, Australia's federally funded employment services provide job matching support and not career guidance. While job matching support may be sufficient for the majority of unemployed job seekers, some groups of adults will require more comprehensive career support, such as mid-career adults who have been displaced after years working in a declining industry, or those who are re-entering the labour market after years spent caregiving or pursuing other types of informal work. These adults could benefit from having their skills assessed, and possibly recognised formally through a recognition of prior learning process. Career guidance can also support them in identifying their transferrable skills, computing skills gaps, and navigating upskilling and reskilling options. Private career guidance may be prohibitively expensive for these groups.

There are some federally funded career guidance programmes for mid-career adults who are unemployed or out of the labour force in Australia, but access is limited. The Mid-Career Checkpoint, Skills Checkpoint for Older Workers and Career Transition Assistance programmes all provide career guidance to mid-career jobseekers. The programmes have a number of strong features, including use of skills assessments and personalised career development roadmaps and financial support for training. The Career Transition Assistance programme also involves employer visits. But these programmes are offered on a small scale, and do not have to be delivered by professional career development practitioners. Rather, they tend to be offered through employment services by counsellors without specialised training in career guidance.

At the state level, Victoria is the only state offering publicly-subsidised career guidance programmes for mid-career jobseekers, and the programme is delivered by professional career development practitioners. As of August 2021, jobseekers in Victoria can be referred to personalised, professional and free career guidance via the Jobs Victoria Career Counsellors Service (see Box 2.7). This programme is delivered by professional career development practitioners. In Victoria, there is a clear separation between the roles of the state-funded career guidance counsellor and federally funded jobactive caseworker, the latter involving performing administrative tasks related to supporting the jobseeker in obtaining benefits.

Box 3.5. Recommendations to support mid-career adults who are unemployed or out of the labour force

- **Scale up publicly provided career guidance programmes that target mid-career jobseekers.** Australia offers career guidance to mid-career jobseekers through the Mid-Career Checkpoint and Checkpoint for Older Workers and some state-level programmes, but capacity and participation are still low, and there is little advertisement of the programmes.

- **Require professionals delivering publicly subsidised career guidance programmes to be listed on the Australian Register of Professional Career Development Practitioners**, as is already the case in Victoria. Such a requirement could increase quality of publicly provided career guidance services for mid-career adults by ensuring that the professionals delivering the service have the required skills and qualifications. This register should be made publicly available.

3.4. Career guidance for mid-career adults who are employed and not facing disruption

Even if they are not facing disruption in their jobs, employed mid-career adults can benefit from career guidance. Analysis of the Australian HILDA survey data shows that the majority of mid-career adults (84%) remain in the same occupation from one year to the next, though not necessarily with the same employer (see Chapter 2). It is important that this group continue to upskill and to progress in their careers even while staying in the same occupation, particularly as the skill needs of a given occupation are susceptible to change with automation and other mega-trends.

Most non-users of career guidance in Australia say that they do not feel the need for it (56%), perhaps because they are employed and established in their career. But if adults viewed career guidance not as a service to access when they "need" it, but as a service to access regularly over the course of their careers in order to maintain their career management skills and improve decision making, then they could be more resilient and better able to respond to labour market shocks. The NCI could better promote lifelong career guidance as a tool to use all along one's career journey, and not only when a person is unemployed or facing an employment transition.

Employed adults who are not facing disruption do not currently have access to publicly subsidised career guidance in Australia, with the exception of the Jobs Victoria Career Counsellors Service which does not base eligibility upon employment status (see Box 2.7). In some OECD countries, employed adults can access publicly subsidised career guidance through career vouchers (such as Flanders (Belgium) or the Netherlands) or via a dedicated public career guidance service (such as France). Another way to scale up public services is to leverage existing programme infrastructure by extending eligibility to mid-career adults. For instance, NCI's School Leavers Information Service, which hires professional career development practitioners to provide career guidance to young people by telephone, could be expanded to include mid-career adults.

Employers can help mid-career workers to understand possible career and learning pathways that exist within their firm. As discussed in Chapter 2, employer-provided career guidance is more common in Australia than in other countries in the SCGA. Employers can help mid-career workers to identify career progression opportunities that exist within the firm, as well as the skill development opportunities offered or supported by the employer.

Career progression depends on mid-career workers first having a clear idea of any skill gaps with respect to their career aspirations. There are two steps involved in computing skill gaps: first, understanding the skills that the worker already has; and second, comparing those skills with those required for the next step in their career.

Understanding the skills that a mid-career worker already has entails making visible the skills they have acquired informally through work experience. As they directly observe employee performance, employers are well placed to support workers in understanding the skills they already have. Recognition of prior learning processes, which exist in most Australian states, are a way for adults to obtain formal recognition for the skills they have acquired informally through work experience or through non-formal training.

A second step in identifying the skills gaps of mid-career workers is to compare their current skills with those required for the next step in their career. Employers should provide transparency to workers about which skills are needed for different roles in their firm. The Australian Skills Classification developed by the National Skills Commission can be a useful tool in this regard, as it sets out the core competencies, specialist tasks and technology tools required for 1 100 occupations in Australia (National Skills Commission, n.d.[3]).

Another way for workers to learn about the different roles in their firm and the associated career pathways is through job rotation and mentorship programmes. Job rotation allows a worker to test drive other roles within the firm and to learn the skills required to perform them. Mentorship programmes connect workers with other employees, often in more senior positions, who teach them new skills and/or provide support in navigating career progression within the firm. While the implementation of such high-performance work practices is ultimately the employer's decision, governments can support employers by providing guidance and disseminating good practice examples. While Australia has funded programmes to raise awareness about high-performance work practices in the past, there are no active programmes in this area. The European Workforce Innovation Network (EUWIN) is an example of how governments can support employers in promoting high-performance work practices (Box 3.6).

Box 3.6. Promoting high-performance work practices within firms

The **European** Workforce Innovation Network (EUWIN) was created in 2013 at the request of the European Commission with the goal to develop and promote the idea of workforce innovation at the European level through knowledge sharing. The network organises international workshops and Europe-wide meetings involving public and private organisations, social partners, policy makers and researchers. An online EUWIN Knowledge Bank provides resources for practitioners and researchers, including articles, case studies and practical guides on how to promote workforce innovation.

According to EUWIN, workplace innovation is built on four elements: i) empowering jobs and self-managed teams, ii) flexible organisational structures, people-centred management practices and streamlined systems and procedures based on trust, iii) systematic opportunities for employee-driven improvement and innovation, and iv) co-created and distributed leadership combined with 'employee voice' in strategic decision-making. These four elements combine to form a system of mutually reinforcing practices that together support the fifth element of workforce innovation: a culture of innovation and organisational and individual resilience.

Building on the success of EUWIN, the European Commission launched targeted implementation projects in the area of workplace innovation. One of these is the INNovaSouth project, which supports small and medium-sized enterprises (SMEs) in Southern Europe to enhance their workplace innovation by increasing the employees' motivation and productivity. Within this project, an Online Manual of Good Practices on Workplace Innovation was developed, providing practical advice to SMEs on how to improve their organisational processes and increase their competitiveness. A call for proposals was also launched under this project that will grant vouchers to selected Greek and Italian SMEs to launch workforce innovation initiatives.

Source: Adapted from OECD (2017[13]), Better Use of Skills in the Workplace: Why it Matters for Productivity and Local Jobs. EUWIN (2016[7]), Your Guide to Workplace Innovation; INNovaSouth (2020[8]), "Project Methodology", https://www.innovasouthproject.eu/methodology/. Adapted from OECD (2021), "Creating Responsive Adult Learning Opportunities in Japan." https://doi.org/10.1787/cfe1ccd2-en.

Box 3.7. Recommendations to support mid-career adults who are employed and looking to progress in their current job/sector

- **Promote the use of high-performance work practices** within firms, including flexible and transparent career and learning pathways, job rotation and mentorship programmes. The NCI could take a lead in these activities.

- **Expand public provision of career guidance to employed mid-career adults, possibly by extending the current telephone-based career guidance service (School Leavers Information Service) to adults.** Employed adults who are not facing disruption do not currently have access to publicly subsidised career guidance across Australia, but could benefit from affordable access to these services over the course of their careers. As the service infrastructure already exists through the School Leavers Information Service, this could easily be extended to include older age groups.

References

Blueprint (2022), *Energy to Digital Growth Education and Upskilling Project (EDGE UP)*, Future Skills Centre, https://global-uploads.webflow.com/5f80fa46a156d5e9dc0750bc/62013a2147ce61c6ef0397ec_FSC-EDGEUP-Final.pdf. [2]

National Skills Commission (n.d.), *Australian Skills Classification*, https://www.nationalskillscommission.gov.au/topics/australian-skills-classification. [3]

OECD (2018), *Getting Skills Right: Australia*, Getting Skills Right, OECD Publishing, Paris, https://doi.org/10.1787/9789264303539-en. [1]

www.ingramcontent.com/pod-product-compliance
Lightning Source LLC
Chambersburg PA
CBHW062029210326
41519CB00060B/7368